THE BA
"LIFE FROM THE OTHER SIDE OF THE FIELD"

By
TYLER CAMPBELL

**FOREWORD BY
EARL CHRISTIAN CAMPBELL**

Table of Contents

ACKNOWLEDGEMENT 2
FOREWORD 3
PROLOGUE 6
CHAPTER 1 "The 12 Yard Line" 11
CHAPTER 2 "Turnovers" 21
CHAPTER 3 "Lost The Ball" 32
CHAPTER 4 "Offsides" 57
CHAPTER 5 "Defense" 67
CHAPTER 6 "Change Of Possession " 72
CHAPTER 7 "UNDRAFTED" 83
CHAPTER 8 "SPECIAL TEAMS" 89
CHAPTER 9 "THE OFF SEASON" 94
CHAPTER 10 "TOUCH-DOWN" 104
CONCLUSION 110
"A Sinner's Prayer" 112
ABOUT THE AUTHOR 113
TESTIMONIALS 114

DEDICATION

To my wife and best friend Shana, thank you for entrusting me with your heart. You will always be the best thing that has ever happened to me. I love you with every fiber of my being and you still give me butterflies. Our children: Messiah, Cheyenne, and Saige, let this book be proof that you can do and be anything you set your heart to. Dad loves you.

ACKNOWLEDGEMENT

Special thank you to my Father, Lord and Savior Jesus Christ, there were many times you could have turned your back on me but you didn't. Instead, you loved me stronger and held me tighter. This book does not have a title without my mentor, Rodney Page. Mr. Page, thank you for being a vessel and bestowing upon me 'Real Life, Reel Talk'. My mother, Reuna and my father Earl, I am forever thankful for teaching me humility, commitment and work ethic. I lean on those core values to this day. Christian, you are the only sibling I have; I love you, man. My mother in law and father in law, Cynthia and Tony, you all have always welcomed me with open arms and accepted me for who I am. I love you both dearly. My sister in law, Thais, you always keep it '100' and I love your children as if they were my own. My brother in law, Obed, always so calm, cool and collected.

Every teammate and coach at all levels, it was a true honor to go to battle, shed blood and cry tears as one in competition. Jumal, you opened up my eyes LYLAB (Love You Like A Brother). Matt, always thankful we sat next to each other in the cafeteria, that moment blessed me with a friend for life. Josh, I appreciate you for always shooting me straight. Bre, I appreciate you for staying on my head and pushing me to do what was so uncomfortable. John, you were the first real friend I ever had and even when I made bad decisions growing up you never turned your back on me. Lastly, Tyler, TX and all who reside in it: I thank you for always being my peace and serving as that bridge over troubled water all of my life.

FOREWORD

My wife and I have been together ever since the ninth grade and after my third MVP ('78, '79, '80) in the (NFL) National Football League we decided to get married. Tyler's mom and I tied the knot in 1980 and began starting a family together.

We have Tyler and his older brother named Earl Christian II. The day my sons were brought into this world my life changed forever for the better. I tell people this all the time, that Earl Campbell's name is a hell of a lot bigger than him. People get life mixed up sometimes with the numbers and fail to see the true person. Number 20 is the guy that won the Heisman, that's one human being or perspective of me. While the man that wore number 34 in the NFL with the Houston Oiler's Franchise, well that's another individual viewpoint.

My sons Tyler and Christian gave me a new perspective on life itself. I would like to say my wife spent the most time with Tyler than me. I'd say that because I was always gone, and constantly working. You heard that old saying about it takes two to tango. It takes two to raise a family. In my situation, my wife, Reuna, she really raised Tyler and Christian.My wife did an amazing job with the boys to say the least.

It's one thing being an athlete, but it's another thing having children while you're a public figure. The spotlight is not only on you but the media attempts to place it on your family as well. Tyler was always able to get better the brighter the lights got. Money, fame, success, and a big name are temporal, anybody can waste it. Anyone can keep riches, any person can blow it, but to be able to see character getting passed down through generations, which you teach your children, in turn they teach their children. That's how this world gets to be a better place. Truly, I had no idea he was watching me the way he did. Tyler represents parts of the best of me, and he took the things I taught him and literally ran with it.

The same hard-core values, morals, and standards I raised my sons with came back to rescue me. When I started having health problems, I got in with these doctors and I thought physicians were next to the Good Lord. I thought what they say goes, and they got me started on those pain pills. Opioids took over my entire life. Losing control, I couldn't get how severe it was at first, but my boys talked to me and thank God they did, because if it hadn't been for my children, I probably wouldn't have never been able to see 65. Tyler and his brother will never have to give me another gift in my lifetime. It is a rarity to find a man like Tyler and not only has he helped me he is still helping to liberate the masses by the power of his story.

My introduction to the condition Multiple Sclerosis came at the hands of my son. I decided to drive over to his apartment and see what the hell was going on with him. That's when I can vaguely remember he had to take his right hand, to move his left arm. Observing Tyler, I noticed when he walked, it was like one leg longer than the other one. Of course, that was a world of awakening to myself because I knew Tyler was a healthy kid. I didn't know that's what MS does to you. I noticed he was stuttering. Nevertheless, there was still an inner strength or tenacity Tyler maintained despite the odds.

I think Tyler is one of the emerging African American voices, and I'm not saying it because he is my son. I just see how God is blessing and put something special deep down inside of him. This may be the next Steve Harvey from a positive standpoint for telling people about how life truly feels. I mean, young people need to hear a positive message and some of us old heads too because Tyler, I don't know where he got it from, but he really doesn't beat around the bush with it. Tyler just gets straight to the point or meets you where you are. I believe he has great chance of having his own nationally syndicated show, talking about 'Real Lyfe, Reel Talk'. I don't know if you heard some of his talks. It's amazing that the young man talks like that, and he can really get your attention, you can hear it in his voice. He doesn't sugar coat it, inside of these pages Tyler will be sharing the truth in the process of holding you accountable. If you plan on going somewhere in this world, you may as well listen to the wisdom that comes out of my son's heart on to these pages.

Whether you are in the basement or at the pinnacle of your success this book is for you. I can think of no one else qualified to show you how to bounce back from being broken than my son Tyler.

PROLOGUE

I looked out at my three children and thought, what am I going to leave behind for them? When it's all said and done what do I want them to remember me as? In the moments proceeding the question that I'd asked myself, it was like God Himself shined a light that illuminated my very being, as it pierced the darkness of my own self resistance. Then the thought hit me like a blindsided tackle write a book, that lasts forever.

I was left with no choice but to realize that it's time to write it because if the Good Lord takes my soul tomorrow, what am I leaving behind for my babies, for them to truly understand their father and what he went through? So, I looked into my family's eyes and I said, "it's time I do it."

Time is truly our most precious commodity. We often find ourselves tricked by the selfies of our youth, while Father Time is steady ticking away. See, I have lost a total of nine family members and friends during COVID. I'm sure without generalizing you've been directly and indirectly impacted by this global pandemic. For me, life became even more precious and sacred. I realized not every day is promised and you tend to take things for granted. We all do, but going through the pandemic and seeing people dying without warning is heart-breaking and a true wake up call.

History can be told or heard. My children can know who they are and the past of their ancestors. Again, if the Good Lord takes my soul tomorrow, at least they will have something tangible that says, "I know my father. I realize he's not here, but he lives in the pages of this book." Those things are something that really tugged on my spirit and I finally yielded.

I'm not determined to be famous but will leave something in the soil for my family. No, it's not about money. You get a better understanding of who you are in the chapters I will reveal here. Legacy is the six letter word that I want to beat like a battle drum in the mind, hearts, and spirits of all who skim the pages.

There are children who do not have their fathers. My dad did not have his own father for very long, and with his father passing, I remember him saying he wished he had more time. The only stories my dad has are very vivid and precise. There are no writings, no journal, barely any pictures. So I want to be better for my family and change the narrative like an audible called at the line of scrimmage.

I really want people, to say, "Oh, he's not that special." And here's what I mean: what I've done, anybody can do. I want people to say, "Great story, but I can too. Matter of fact, I can do it better. I can go further, I can go faster, and I can make an even greater impact." I really and truly want people to say, "He's not that special. Why not me? I got blood in my veins just like you do. I have to put in my work. I have to put on my shoes and go to work just like you do. I'm married and have children like you. I've come through ups and downs just like you." But I want people to say, "Man, why not me?" And also, "What is so special about Tyler Campbell? I can do this thing too."

If you're reading this page right now, just know despite the odds, you can. You are equipped with everything that you already need, despite your race, gender, background, and color. Whether you come from money, or you don't have it you are still fully loaded with a divine purpose. It's all embedded and it's still in you, but you have to tap into a gift and you have to tap into your purpose in life. When you recognize those things, my brothers and sisters, can't nothing stop you. Nothing can derail you when you understand who you are, your self-worth, your gift and your purpose, because you tapped into what the divine Man up above gave you.

For me the biggest things that I've learned, because I've been going through therapy as a man for the past half year is, addressing and being able to really tap in and be vulnerable. So for me, the vulnerability, transparency, and authenticity are the three things that come to mind, because I feel like I can't tap into the hearts and minds of anybody else without opening up about some of my weaker moments in life. In the proceeding chapters it is my hope that you will laugh, cry, think, and be transformed by the unedited version of me.

It's crazy because I think everybody always taps into Earl Campbell's son. They say, "You're Earl Campbell's son" but people don't want to hear Tyler's story. They don't even address me by my name. Most people catch 'I'm Earl Campbell's son', so much so that they forget to understand that I am Tyler. People ask me why I approach my disease the way that I do, why I have the perspective, why I have the belief, the energy, and the hope. Oftentimes, I don't get the chance to tell people a lot of who I am and why I approach life the way that I do. Inside of this book I'm giving you total access to the lessons that I learned along the way.

Mostly people would always want me as a speaker to fast forward to the Multiple Sclerosis and get to, I guess, the beautiful part of the story. On stage, I'm glued to a criterion for a business model or function. I am held to a message that mainstream wants to be conveyed. I'm grateful, it is my job as a speaker to serve you the masses that message. On the other hand, with my book, I actually get to pull back the curtains to my left to tell how I got to this place and why I have my belief. During our time together I'll share why I have my faith and how that changed my life. I get to communicate the story that I've been longing to voice for 35 years of my life. I finally get to articulate my truth and guess what? Nobody can stop me.

There's one person who needs to read my book and I'm just trying to reach that one person. Can I let you in on a huge secret? That one person is you. I've also got in my mind a black teenage boy, somewhere in this country. I see his face, I don't know his name, but he's lost. He has incredible gifts, but he doesn't know it. He's the person I'm trying to write this book for. I see him.

From cover to end, I want to tell that boy that his uniqueness is actually in that thing that he feels is a plaque over his soul. What he's going through is not his worst enemy. I've discovered through trials and countless errors that you don't have to want to cry out to change that 'thing', because that 'thing' inside will transform you. The struggle that you feel makes you so different or brands you as an outcast, is actually the bridge to your platform. The difference or uniqueness is going to give you the stage to tap into the hearts and minds of people across the world. If you're looking at yourself as an outsider, as if you don't fit and if you think you're not like your brother or father and that your footsteps are different I am sure, you're going to make just as much of an impact in your own way. You're not going to have to carry a football to do it. Ask me how I know? I want to encourage all that pick this book up. You will have the husband, you'll have the wife, and you are going to have the kids. You are going to have the love. I know you may have wanted to make an impact in sports. Trust me, you're going to make an impact. It's just not the way that you thought it was going to happen. Sports was the only way that I thought I could achieve success in life. I didn't know any better. Boy, was I wrong.

Through life's ups and downs, I discovered that smiling is one of the easier things you can do. My secret sauce or superpower is my heart. The reason I say my heart is because my heart has a direct connection to the Man up above. You see, because our brain has the amygdala in it. The amygdala releases your emotions. It's been scientifically proven that the amygdala in the brain works conjunctively with the heart. The heart and brain must align for the body to properly function. The brain and the heart are tied together. Realize this, the brain can't go with the trigger unless it hits from the heart first. Putting it in proper prospective, I have an establishment and a relationship with the Lord up above and He taps into my heart strings that allows me to walk into any room or any situation and already claim the victory long before it has even manifested. When people see me, they see a smile, and they feel a level of connection.

I understand whole heartedly the purpose and the calling that the Man up above put on me and it lives through my heart. The pulse of my heart is what people feel. When you are having a conversation with someone, you know that they are speaking, not only to you, but they are speaking through you. What I think people feel most when they interact with me, they'll notice that it comes from a level of love that is different. I'll give you my heart and I'll wear it on my sleeve with pride. It has been broken many, many times before. It doesn't deter me from loving. I'll give you my heart in every word of this book.

I'm committed to walking you through my childhood and I am dedicated to leading you towards some of the darkest and loneliest times of my life. I know what manhood looks like now, but I did not know this when my journey began. I did not understand what a man really and truly was, until I got into my early thirties. Now I am compelled to opening up about things that I always felt like nobody wanted to hear. I'm in a safe place to not question or worry about what other people think about my words. I want to give you my triumph, but I also want to give you my failures and my faults. I've never been more ready to share my life when the ball came out.

CHAPTER 1 "The 12 Yard Line"

I found that my family name doesn't conclude of whom or what I am. Writing an autobiography is hard. I've got to look through my past like pages in a book when I have always tried my best not to remember it. Sometimes I like to wonder what I would have done if I hadn't been diagnosed with a disease that changed my life. Even though the answer is obvious, I still wonder if there were any other ways. As a person who lacked confidence, it pains me to think about many incidents. Now, nobody can stop me when I scream to the world. If I die today, what am I going to leave behind? That is what I thought before starting an autobiography about my life.

I was born in Houston, but grew up in Austin, Texas on the west side, in a community they call Westlake. A real affluent community with barely any black people in it. At first glance I thought that this was a normal portrait of the world.

My father Mr. Earl Campbell, NFL Hall of Famer was the official state hero of Texas. There are four state heroes in the state of Texas: Sam Houston, Stephen F. Austin, David Crockett, and the fourth is my father, Earl Campbell. I got my name from his hometown Tyler, Texas and my brother is Earl Jr.

My father is a living legend listed in the capital declaration official hero of the state of Texas for playing the game of football. He had a hard time in his life but he escaped the grips of poverty long before he broke free of a tackle in the National Football League.

If there was such a thing as rock bottom, he climbed from underneath it, but he never talks about all those things. My father and mom both came from rural East Texas.

I had to recognize the world that I was stepping and living in was a world my parent's didn't grow up in. Also, I had to discover that they had survived life of humble beginnings paving the way for my brother and I, however we were living life on a different side of the tracks than what they grew up on. Mom and dad truly started from the bottom with sincere determination and grit that I only could aspire to scratch the surface of.

In 1991, dad started Earl Campbell Foods which sold custom made sausage. My dad vowed without flinching that he was going to make his sausage brand something that will surpass what he'd done on the football field. Big words from a Hall of Famer. It's always a legacy of winning with my dad, even if he was betting on himself and set his mindset on breaking personal records.

See, I come from a foundation of entrepreneurial workers. Mom, dad, and my grandmother all worked for themselves. They showed me that you can build businesses from the ground up. I saw my parents build firsthand as a kid and my mind was exposed to that from an early age. I was beyond blessed to have an entrepreneurial blueprint handed down to me. Truly, I felt that there wasn't anything my parents couldn't do when they set their minds to it.

I've seen the set up and breakdown of many demos in grocery stores. My dad didn't rely on others to put in the work; he was the face of the brand but also would roll up his sleeves and do the dirty work. My father would be in there with Wrangler jeans and his cowboy boots, demoing his own product. He could have hired someone but felt he was the best person to market his company. Dad brought the same winning and leadership mentality to the company as he had manifested on the football field. If his team or company needed to score, my dad would want the ball in his hands.

On the other hand, it wasn't all business or football with my dad. Earl Campbell was a true family man who loved to spend time with his kids. Every Friday growing up, my father would take us out to eat. My brother and I loved this one on one time with our dad. As we got a little bit older and were in elementary school, he even let us bring our friends along with us to dinner. Going out to eat with dad, my brother, and friends are my most precious childhood memories. These moments are embedded in my heart. Sometimes we'd go to burger joints, like Dirty Martin's Place, but then he would take us to Tokyo Steakhouse which is now, Benihana. For us as kids this was better than going to the circus, the chefs were cooking food right there in front of you doing the tricks with an onion. We were beyond excited and intrigued every time we went to Tokyo Steakhouse. People were always coming up to take pictures with Earl Campbell. I'd grown used to that side of dad who posed for fan photos, but I felt like I got the best part of it. Truly, I savored the best part of my father that nobody else saw. My dad was and is more to me than signed memorabilia and impromptu photos. Earl Campbell was my father and my hero beyond the helmet.

Dad was obsessed with being a father because he didn't have his for very long. My father's dad died very early in his life. Dad didn't ever say but I felt like he was robbed of the father and son bond. So everything that he wanted or he dreamed of what a father was supposed to be for him, he poured that and then some into my brother and I. I'm forever grateful for what my dad imparted into us boys. Like I said before, I was named after dad's hometown and my brother's is my father's namesake. We both got the lion's share of the man behind the legend.

My mother Reuna, who was the first generation in her family to go to college, was a strong beautiful and bright lady. She was the loudest one, chanting and rooting me on in the stands and everything.

All the kids used to love her. My momma was that momma at the games leading her own chants "rebound, get it, get it, rebound, get it, get it." My mom would make up her own cheers and brought high energy to the games my brother and I played in. On top of that, my mom's grace and class were impeccable and second to none.

Mom was an entrepreneur in her own right. She had a clothing store called Boy O Boy, off of Far West Boulevard. Mom is and will always be that solid rock in my life. As my brother and I got older and busier, my mother had to get out of 'Boy O Boy' because her own boys were taking up so much of her time and dad was on the road. Dissolving her business to put the needs of her children first was just one of the many sacrifices she made throughout my life. Mom was the pillar of the family, loving but no, she didn't tolerate nonsense. It has always been when you get in trouble, you'd go see dad. He's going to ease it up, dad is going to cover for you. For mom, it's all business, no games.

It broke my heart growing up because I had to sit there and watch my dad's body deteriorating. The best way to describe it was to imagine seeing your superman crippled by the thing he loved and mastered. Boy, I remember all those cries at night, him hollering out in pain, the back surgeries, crippling arthritis, the knee operations. All the dark stuff that dad had to go through behind the scenes and away from the limelight. We lived through it every day. I saw my father crying because he had to ask for help to even turn over in his bed or to be bathed. I saw a man's pride broken because he had to ask for help. This mountain of a man was reduced by his frailties and those things broke my heart as well because I know he literally put everything he had into his body to change the course of not only his family but to break a generational curse and to set a new precedent.

During my teens, I attended Westlake High School, the same

school as Drew Brees, Chris Mihm and Nick Foles, a perennial powerhouse in the state of Texas. I'm so proud to say Westlake was my high school. Westlake is a football dynasty, consistent playoff runners, and state champions. Westlake High school was a place of bittersweet memories.

I learned things about my dad through my friend's parents and the lenses they saw him through. Every time I stepped into someone's home, everyone knew who I was. I was always the only black kid there. When I looked around and figured out that I was different from those around me I felt ugly. Felt like I existed, for God knows why and didn't have any direction. Some of you reading this page right now can relate to being stuck in the unknown. You know the lost feeling of not knowing who you are at all? I felt afraid to tell my parents because I already thought I was letting them down because I knew they had high expectations for me. I was a Campbell and I could clearly see the end zone, but for some reason I couldn't cross the line of scrimmage.

I couldn't make it across the invisible line of scrimmage because I was getting stalemated by the internal walls that blocked my identity. It was bigger than the football field I played on. See, I didn't know who I was and was aimlessly searching for my own identity. I thought I knew but didn't have a clue as a teen.

On the surface I had a somewhat normal teenage life. I liked to look at comic books, play video games and loved watching BET. I couldn't wait for Rap City to come on with Joe Clair and Big Tigger as the years went on. Football turned everything upside down as everything became about the game off football. Winning and performing raced in my mind like sirens on the top of an ambulance.

At the same time, I started to become more and more aware that there's not too many people around my surroundings that look like me and I began having many inner thoughts. I can remember thinking, 'who am I really?' I'd ask myself internally, 'Tyler where are you headed in life?' When people in my environment looked at me, I felt like I could hear them saying, "You're Earl Campbell's son, of course you can play ball." It was if I'd had no other choice but carry the torch or like they use as a football terminology "carry the rock."

When those football pads started cracking and life started setting in on me for the very first time, I had no idea. I saw that there is 'opportunity'. You know that it may not be good right now but you are so close to figuring it out whatever that 'thing' is.

And so, I believed that football was going to create my identity, it would keep me safe and it would create the circle for me within that in-crowd. So, I was going to follow my blockers and use the field to keep me grounded.

My past generation was full of ball players that also included my brother, Christian. So I had to be better than good and average just wouldn't cut it. Even though my father didn't tell me to follow his path, I felt that is what I was supposed to do. It was my duty to run behind the legacy he left for me. I trained hard trying to be the best but was depressed as I couldn't live up to the hype. The truth of the matter is, the pressure was not coming from the family, it was something that I built within myself; it was my own self-manufactured world of many pressures and expectations. Imagine putting yourself under a weight bench and adding an unsurmountable amount pounds, yet trying to lift them. Well that's exactly what it felt like I was doing to myself.

I didn't have to impress my parents like some kids I knew because they loved me for me with or without a football in my hands. Here I am with two parents and even some of my cousins wished they had a loving family, like mine. Yet, I felt like I had to prove something when nothing could have been farther from the truth.

I said to myself, "if I don't play football then I won't necessarily fit in the society like I did before." I scored two touchdowns in my first game as a 7th grader at Hill Country Middle School, against Leander. And from that point on the rest of the season went downhill.

On the field I wasn't fast nor was I agile. I was so athletically behind that there was a terrible difference between the ball and me. I could feel the vibe or state of shock from coaches and even from my teammates. Needless to say, I got benched that year. My position in football was taken right before my eyes. I was playing scared. I didn't want to block and I tried my best not to hit anyone. I remember my father telling me, "You can't play scared. If you play scared, you're going to get hurt." Often, I found myself cuddled up in a world that was filled with disappointment, anxiety pressure and sorrow.

It was the beginning of realizing that, I had never thought of my own identity that was filled with my wishes and dreams. Just building that world for myself believing that playing ball is what I'm supposed to do. Blinded by football, I ignored all the things that I loved about my life. I stopped reading those little comic books. Truth be told, I forfeited parts of myself earlier on to pursue football.

Everything started to unfold when this 11-year old boy turned 12 during the school year. I was in seventh grade but I was supposed to be in sixth grade. So puberty-wise, I was always behind everybody. Again stuck behind the 12-yard line. Attending Hill Country Middle School at 12 years old, was the beginning of seventh grade football and the beginning of my football journey.

As a black kid, I had spent many nights at white people's homes. So my parents were intrigued, "What was your night like? What did you all eat?" I had to understand that although they had lived through life, I was living life on a different side of the tracks than what they grew up in. Coming back home from a friend's house back then felt like show and tell.

I would love to say that my life in a predominately white environment was peaceful and serene but that wouldn't be accurate. There was a gentleman by the name of James Byrd who was from Jasper, Texas, which is in East Texas. I was in middle school when James was followed by white supremacists. The three individuals abducted James Byrd, beat him profusely and then dragged him to his death behind their pickup truck. This act of hatred was gruesome and heartless to say the least. My world was rocked. At that time, President Clinton was coming to East Texas, where all my family members are from. Therefore, it became a huge deal.

That was the first time I honestly felt like, I'm *different*. And I realized, what happened to James, could happen to me. I would even have nightmares about it. This was the first time I recall being afraid because of the color of my skin. After the horrific chain of events occurred, I started to look at the world through a different lens. However, at the same time, I didn't know how I was supposed to go to about it. I didn't know how to approach my parents, what therapy was or if I should have talked to a counselor. Having nowhere to go get help, began the process of me as a young kid really internalizing a lot of the stuff that I saw and felt. Voices conducted like a symphony in my head that repeated the chorus of denial. Don't talk about this topic. That's emotional stuff. Nobody cares about that type of stuff. You've got to get yourself together. Get ready to play football. Nonetheless, the cruelty that happened to James was frequently appearing in my mind. Although I needed to get ready for football these critical thoughts were embedded in my mind heading into the school year.

I always played yard football as a kid with my friends John, Andy and William. They used to call me the 'Black terminator' because I always had so much anger. The crazy thing is I never understood where it came from. That being said, playing in pads for the first time in seventh grade was a different beast. I was terrified and I was like, "What is this? This isn't like yard football. This stuff actually hurts." I told nobody that I was terrified. I tried to make everything mimic my father, walking in his footsteps was a priority for me. I even acquired the number 20. My brother was a big fan of Deion Sanders, so he wore number 2 when he played ball. It was the number Deion made famous when he was at Florida State University. I remember telling my dad that I was going to be just like him. That meant wearing my dad's University of Texas at Austin number 20. It was an honor to wear my dad's number.

Dad and mom went to college and it was expected that the next generation would follow suit. I saw what you can do if you also take care of things academically. I started to struggle in the classroom in the fourth grade with reading comprehension, but that spread more into math and science as I advanced to middle school. I would begin to lose focus when I looked around in the classroom and discovered everybody else was getting A's and B's on the same assignments. Some of my classmates would end up getting into Ivy League colleges and other affluent schools. There was no reason why I couldn't but I used to get caught looking at everybody else's stuff and started to stop focusing on myself. I thought I was an incapable learner and I couldn't learn the same way as them. My schoolwork was greatly affected due to loss of focus. My brother used to have to go to tutoring and I ended up doing the same. It wasn't that I didn't get the information, I just wasn't as quick. I used to start looking out at the class like, 'How the heck, are these people getting this information and I'm not? What's going on?' Then when you start to get frustrated you start to just give up. For me, C's became acceptable. Average seemed easy to manage. I used to excuse it because, oh, I played sports and being a student athlete is tough. It used to drive the family nuts. Being on the 12-yard line of the field is a good thing if you are driving in for a touchdown. On the other hand, if you are stuck in the Red Zone (12-yard line) and can't get a score you have wasted a trip.

Chapter 2 "Turnovers"

"No quitting, whatever you do give it everything that you have because tomorrow is not promised to anybody," is what my father had told me. Quitting has never been an option or a Plan B. Go hard or go home was not just a motto but encoded in my genes. I live by this code.

My brother was the one who said, "You got to work for what you want Tyler. I know you think I just wake up and just do the stuff but I do actually work really hard." My brother was the epitome of what an elite athlete looked like. He used to put a heck of a lot of time in on the east side of town. Christian was 16 years old when he was second in the state of Texas, 5A high school division, in the 200 meters as a sophomore. If you looked up speed in the dictionary you'd see my brother's picture right next to it. He was dual sport athlete, played wide receiver on the football team and ran track. He was vastly becoming a high school standout. His scholarship mail was starting to come in droves from colleges from all over the country. He was even featured in the notorious Dave Campbell Football Magazine, which is like the bible down in Texas. Everyone reads it prior to the start of the football season. The guy was amazing, and I loved watching him compete from the stands. I was so proud of him and his success.

What many didn't know is that behind my brother's talents and accomplishments on the field, he had an even fiercer work ethic. For example, Christian would workout on the eastside of town with a gentleman by the name of Carmet Kiara. Carmet would have athletes run a massive hill where the Old Anderson High School once stood. What took his speed and endurance to another level was training with the Austin Striders Track Club, led by Howard and Harvey Ware. My brother started to show me that if you want to change, you got to really work on it and forget the video games and everything else. Christian said, "You got to get out in this Texas heat and work at it. And you can control your work ethic. You can't always control what happens around you but you can control Tyler and what you give to something. And whatever you choose to do, I don't care, just give it your all."

That summer coming into eighth grade, I started working out with Carmet Kiara. I changed my football number from 20 to 32, which would be the jersey number that I would wear for the rest of my career.

I got my shot due to a sudden change of events. One of our starting running backs got hurt in the middle of the year, so I got to start. He had broken his hand and fingers. I got switched from full back to running back and it just flowed from there. Ooh, it was my time and I seized the moment. I took over the running back position and I made the best of carrying the (rock) football.

If you know anything about football you know the momentum of the game changes due to **turnovers**. Just like that, my coach took me from playing fullback, always being the blocker, and moved me to the position of running back. Now I felt like everything I did became a part of the sport I was playing, football became an important part of life for me.

In eighth grade, I had a girlfriend named Talia. It was like I was becoming popular and things were falling into place for me. Going to high school as a freshman, where my brother was a senior, everybody knew Christian Campbell as he had his own swag. He was truly 'the man' in high school. I was walking in my big brother's footsteps. I didn't mind that at all because I looked up to him. My brother's football team that year lost to Midland Lee High School in the 5A state Championship, a team that featured two Parade High School All Americans and future NFL draft picks in Cedric Benson and Eric Winston. At that time in my life, I was so happy to be where my brother was. I was so proud to be near him. I'm seeing up close the way my brother walked and how he mingled with his classmates. Everybody knew CC (Christian Campbell). Sadly, my brother didn't win the state championship that year in track like he wanted. It didn't matter at that time, I was his little brother and living under his shadow.

Christian knew he was going to college at the University of South Carolina for track. I saw all of his letters in the mail from UCLA, Kentucky to LSU and everywhere in between just to put it into perspective. I was so incredibly happy for him. My big brother was making moves and was college bound. That meant a lot to us but on a greater scale our parents were ecstatic.

As a result of another **turnover,** I arrive at Westlake High School where I get switched back to the fullback position. Midseason, I got rotated back into the line-up to running back. The starter had become sidelined due to academic issues. It's funny how God works and thanks to my coaches Jeff Montgomery and Zach Brockman for giving me a shot. Just like that, I am making my first start at running back as a freshman on the freshmen team at Westlake High School. Talk about the mixture of emotions during this short stretch of time. To top my first start off, I returned a kick-off for a touchdown against a team called the Hays Rebels.

This was a huge deal for me and a confidence booster for many reasons. The Hays Rebels played the song 'Dixie' when they scored touchdowns over the loud speakers. Yes, you read it right, they would play 'Dixie'. Their colors were red, white and blue. Here I am, this

African American teenager returning the kick-off for the touchdown. It didn't stop there. Later in the game we ran a play called Red Right 36 Reverse Left. When I took the ball on the reverse and saw that everybody else on the defensive side was flowing left, I felt daylight and cut back in the B gap behind the left guard, the opposite way to the side-line and didn't stop running full speed until I reached the end zone. During the game, I had well over some 200 yards between returns and rushing.

Little did I realize me scoring was going to lead to another **turnover** in my high school season. The next thing I know, Ron Schroeder, the head varsity football coach, approached me that Friday when I was walking along to class and asked, "Man, you ever thought about playing varsity football?" Though a little surprised, I replied, "I'm going to play varsity football. I would love to play." It was a big deal because our high school was so prominent and to be a sophomore on varsity was a big deal. Each year only a few incoming sophomores get called up to varsity. This was a chance of a lifetime because this was an opportunity to play with the best of the best. Remember, Westlake High School was known for producing great teams and I was going to be on one of them. Just like that an amazing and difficult freshman football season started and passed. It was an absolute blur to me.

Right after my fall freshmen season ended, I was catapulted into the varsity off-season program that spring. That meant as soon as that football season is over with, you as a freshman begin working out with the varsity football team. In Texas, we have an intensive period for sports. That's right, football had its own period. Football in the state of Texas is serious business. It's like we had two practices. I remember my first day in the off season program. I knocked on the portable window of my old language arts class. I was letting people know I used to be in your class, but now I'm out here working out with the varsity. It was like I had found my identity and it was my coming out party. Although I was on the Varsity

Team, I was still a year younger than everybody my grade. As a freshman, I was turning 14 but in my head I was growing up. At the same time my girlfriend Talia moved to Arkansas at the end of the year, which was heart-breaking for me. We even used to wear the same basketball Jersey number 42. Then before you knew it she was gone as quick as I had found her.

Westlake High School Football was everything but I had to get knee surgery before the start of my sophomore year and I missed the entire football season. Once again an unexpected **turnover** would change the course of my season.

I know the senior girls had to be thinking, "We come to your house and decorate your room every Thursday before Friday night lights, but you don't play a single down." There were about four other sophomores, I think, that made varsity with me and the other cats got in the game. For the first time in my life, I developed an identity or what I presumed to be an identity. Then it was gone. At that moment I felt like I didn't fit in. A knee injury took football away for the very first time. Surgery on my right knee made a blank page in my life. Sometimes I could even see a question mark in it.

Junior year was a different story. I was blessed to walk out of the season with impressive accolades. This was largely because of the hard work and dedication of my teammates and coaches. Also, I had put in the work that off season. I was hungry and ready. Isn't it funny how being away from the things you love can ignite a fire within you. I walked out of that junior season, ranked the 32nd best Junior Class prospect overall in the state of Texas. I was the number two Junior class Running Back in the state. I was shocked, I didn't think of myself as that good. NFL Pro Bowler and future Hall of Famer Adrian Peterson was the number one Junior running back and number 1 overall prospect in the state of Texas. Man, was it a talented class. I felt privileged to be a part of it and overtime, I embraced it.

You can imagine the looks you got from people when you're ranked number 2 at your position. See, I was coming into my own and experiencing the joys that came along with being a sought after athlete. Fame, recognition, and notoriety. I got a new girlfriend. She made me happy, I smiled more. I fell in love and it felt great.

In my junior year, I was on top of my game and I literally thought I was invincible. At 16 years old, I walked into my parent's room and I told them, they don't have to worry about paying for school for me. My promise to them was that I'd get a full ride scholarship. Getting a scholarship was my gift back to them. It was a way of saying you did a great job raising me and now it is my time to honor you.

Soon, mail started to come in from all over. My first offer for scholarship was San Diego State University, followed by Baylor University. Then the mail started coming from Missouri, Notre Dame, Arizona State University and even Coach Nick Saban who was at LSU at the time. Due to the recent chain of events, I was now on top and things were finally turning over for me. It was at this point I knew I could play ball at the next level.

This was all new to me, I wasn't used to success. I didn't know how to react to the word 'success'. Let's just say, I wasn't really prepared for 'success'. I never truly prepared for the recruiting process or the phone calls from recruiting agencies that wanted interviews. Coaches were now personally calling to speak to me. It was like I was dreaming but reality was undeniable. At the same time, I was still going through tutoring, specifically for Latin. I remember talking to Mark Stoops from the University of Arizona at the time. When he called the house phone I had to tell my tutor, "Hold on, I got to talk."

It felt so good to be wanted and sought after. These were new feelings for me and the negative to them was that I felt invincible. Nothing could stop me, I was on my way up. Despite not knowing fully which way was up, I was convinced that I was on my way. Well, like it has been said, the only thing that can ultimately stop a person would be themselves.

Living in a society where people had access to money, alcohol, and even drugs, I started drinking Seagram's 7 Gin and it began to be my 'go to'. I wasn't necessarily after the taste, I just wanted the sensation that alcohol gave me, a feeling of 'getting lost.' Alcohol made me feel like I was right at home and nothing could mess up my flow.

In my extended family, everybody drinks. So I was supposed to have a few. I never really liked weed as much because I smoked it one time and I felt like my Adam's apple was about to come out of my mouth. I was paranoid and freaking out. In the off season, I rode this wave of being on cloud nine because I knew college was taken care of. "Just don't get hurt next year" is what I kept telling myself. "Just do half of what you did last year and it's going to be cool".

Four months after my 16th birthday in the month of February, I made a poor decision to get drunk before a high school basketball game. We were playing our cross town rivals, Austin High.

There's another guy on my football team, named Steven. He was a tremendous athlete and would become the first black scholarship football player from Westlake. He ended up playing college football at the Ohio University. We were the only two brothas on the team. I always loved and respected the fact that Steven wore his hair braided. I wanted cornrows but my mom wasn't having it. I remember going past Steven that night in the gym and he could smell the alcohol on my breath. It was the rare look that Steven gave me that said it all. In my mind I think he's saying, "Man, I can't believe you're doing this here. I wouldn't even do this here. You're showing up to a gymnasium, sold out crowd and you're drunk? And you're like one of the few black people out here and you think you'll go unnoticed?"

During the game, the police officers made their way to the section I was seated in and they pulled me out of the stands in front of a sold-out crowd. A life that I dreamed, completely changed in an instance as I turned it over.

I was 16 years old when I showed up drunk to Austin High's campus. That night, I lied to the policeman. Even though I knew that he knew that I was drunk, I still denied it. The police officers escorted me out the gym but they did me a solid. They put me in a room by myself. Then they asked me if I had anyone that I could call to come and take me home. I decided to call my teammate, Hunter. In the meantime, they were trying to get me to sober up. The police officers truly went out of their way to help me. Hunter came and got me when the game was over and drove me to another party. Go figure, I'm still drinking because I'm saying to myself, "See, I can't be touched, Right?"

The next morning, I drove to Barton Creek Country Club like always. I had learned from my brother that if you drink, your next destination is the steam room. 'Go hit the steam room and sweat the alcohol out'. Everything I thought I knew was making matters worse but was too young to see it at the time.

School and off season practice were on the following Monday. I loved the times when office aides came to class, because that always meant someone was getting out early. That day, the office aide came with a pink slip and turned it over to the teacher, who just so happened to be our defensive coordinator, Coach Long. Coach then brought the slip to my desk. I looked at the pink slip which was noted for me to report to the principal's office. I think my coaches already knew what I had done. Everybody knew what I had done, I wasn't invincible in reality only in my made-up mentality.

No lie this was the longest walk I've ever taken in my life. When I sat down with the principal, I saw a glimpse of his assistant. I knew things were serious based on all the butterflies tossing around in the pit of my stomach. In truth, I have never visited the principal's office before. The next words out of my principal's mouth surprised me, "You've got to go to our AEP program. And it's the alternative education program. You got to finish the school year out there."

"Why?" I asked in total disbelief and shock.

"Tyler, you came drunk to a basketball game on a school campus. Do you know the consequences of your actions? You are a minor that consumed alcohol on a school campus. It's a triple threat. We'll be contacting your parents later."

I didn't talk to anyone, as a matter of fact I felt like a walking zombie. The last bell rang and I visited my friend Kailey at her home. Kailey was a good friend of mine and someone I could trust. We had been going to school together since the 2nd grade.

Before I realized it, I blurted, "Kailey, my momma, Reuna Campbell is about to kill me. Alright, go ahead and write my obituary. The funeral, the death warrant, and everything in between."

"It can't be that bad," Kailey said.

"She may be sweet to you but, my mom is going to kill me" I replied.

After an hour or so I went back to my home and decided to tell my mother what happened before anyone else. I cleared my throat as I entered the kitchen. I was nervous. But I had to do it. She dropped her pen as I started blurting out words. Then only did I notice, she was paying bills. I said reluctantly, "Momma I went to Austin High, and I got drunk. If you haven't noticed already, your phone's getting ready to ring. I got drunk. I got to go through this thing called the Alternative System for the district." I peeked at her bracing for her response to the news and saw tears rolling down her cheeks. No words at first just streaks of tears streaming down like rain on a car windshield during a storm. I took a step backward trying to grasp at the situation. I expected her to yell at me. Maybe it would better than making her cry. She sobbed as she said, "I can't look at you right now." I stood there as I watched her tears continue to wet the glass kitchen table. At that moment I knew what it was. I've got everything handed to me. As a first-generation college student, my parents worked so hard to provide a better life for me. All they asked is for me to stay clear of the police. I got things that my mom and dad didn't always have, such as food, clothes and stability. I had opportunities, resources, and a legacy to follow. It was shocking of how easy it was for me to turn it all over for some alcohol.

My mom was completely heartbroken by my actions. My pops came home. He tried his best to get home to beat me telling my mom first so he could buffer it, but I had already told her. To this day, I have never seen my mom cry the way she did that evening in the kitchen in 2003. That is still an image I can never get out of my head.

Life at this time was nothing short of a constant emotional roller coaster. I have it and I then don't have it. Turnover after turnover. Pops came to see me in my room the next day and said, "I've got to tell you something but you are not going to like this. You know all those schools that called you. This is what you got to do. You got to call every single person. Even the people who didn't offer you a scholarship. If they don't pick up leave a message, you got to call each of them and tell them what you got in trouble for."

He told me that he was raising men to be honest underneath his roof and how important character is as a man, that my character is going to outlast anything that I do. While making these calls, my inner thoughts turned into spoken words, "When they see Tyler

Campbell, what do you want them to say?" I remember leaving many messages. Coaches never called back. I remember leaving Georgia Tech a voicemail and in the middle of the voicemail, I think I might've even said, "Tyler, what are you doing?" It was like, literally every call I made I felt like I was speaking my future away.

Truth be told I never once got mad at my dad. I knew what he expected me to do was the moral thing to do. I'm not upset with him at all still to this day. I think it was the greatest lesson he could have ever taught me. On the other hand, to actually live it and to see opportunity slowly fade little by little, needless to say it was a very humbling experience.

I had to tell the truth. I had to be a stand-up man. Mom didn't talk to me for quite an amount of time. When the time came to break her silence she grabbed the book, 'The Purpose Driven Life'. She doesn't even remember it now. I'll never forget reading it every night. I had Rick Warren's 'Purpose Driven Life' in my hand more than a football during this time. I swear she probably sprinkled some holy water on me one night. She was really worried but she says that to this day, "I don't remember that." I replied, "Mom, we had to do it every night. 'Purpose Driven Life' with Rick Warren." I know that book like the back of my hand from turning over the pages. I firmly believe that book was the beginning of the transformation in my life that bought me closer to Christ. I looked forward nightly to understanding Him better. I wanted to know His purpose for my life. On a Palm Sunday in 2003 at Mt. Olive Baptist Church, I couldn't hold back the curiosity anymore. I gave my life to Him that day. It's crazy because I don't even remember how I got from the back of the church to the front to declare that I wanted to be baptized. I just know that He called so I answered and I was made all the better because of it.

CHAPTER 3 "Lost The Ball"

So I'm calling these college head coaches and telling them what I had done wrong. You can imagine then the phone started ringing a lot less. It got to a point that the phone stopped ringing completely. I don't know if it was because of my troubles or other things that were beyond my control.

Based on disciplinary restrictions, I was not allowed to be with the student population for the remainder of my junior year. I'm now completing my course work in the alternative high school system. I remember reading a letter from Notre Dame, the following week. That was a huge deal because Tyrone Willingham was an African American head coach. I thought to myself, 'If I can get a degree from Notre Dame and have the opportunity to play for a black head coach', that would be a special college experience. It really got me excited! Please understand, a black head coach was something I never had before. As a matter of fact, the closest thing was a Sunday school teacher. So I'm like, 'You can go to Notre Dame'. I remember like it was yesterday reading this handwritten letter addressed to me from Coach. I am facing the walls in this alternative room and I began to ponder to myself, "How in the world am I going to get out of here and to Notre Dame or any other school, for that matter?" It's like I was reading the opportunities, but with the barriers in place, how would all of this be possible? The handwritten letters are what I longed to read, not the typed ones. At that time handwritten ones had more meaning because in your mind you think, 'Yo, that's coming from coach'. Being 16 years old, you didn't know that the coach's secretaries were the ones writing those letters. To an athlete, there's a difference between a handwritten letters in the recruitment process than a typed out one. Typed mail was mass produced and not as significant. Handwritten were the letters that asked you, "How's your brother Christian? How is your mom, Reuna?" Those letters from coaches felt personable and not business only. They showed you that they were doing their homework. Daily I'm reading all this stuff behind the walls of the alternative system. How would I go from where I was to keeping a dream alive? I see the opportunity but I've **lost the ball.** Prospects were still coming my way but how would I obtain them and keep my play alive. At times it felt like I was so close but yet so far. Days I swear, life felt like it was taunting me. Trying to keep a grasp of the chain of events was the part that really used to get me. You know you can play football but how?

My classmates were going to Harvard, Yale, Dartmouth, University of Texas, SMU, and Georgia, on scholarships. Here I am, the token athlete who had every opportunity and now is slowly starting to fizzle behind closed doors. The facts were that I was the number two junior running back prospect in the state of Texas, and the number 32 prospect overall. The Midlands Sweet 66, which consisted of the best athletes from (TX, CO, NE, MO, KS and OK), had me ranked the 7th best running back in the region and 52nd overall. This was all according to Rivals.com the elite high school recruiting database during my era. Today, people go by ESPNs rankings. I still have the article to this day. Six-time NFL Pro Bowler Defensive End, Calais Campbell, was even on that list at #41, can you believe it? I'm like, "Man, Calais Campbell is still playing football in the NFL today." This was a time where my ability had emerged. Opportunity was presenting itself, but I didn't know how I was going to be able to seize it. The Lord was working on something because even after all these accolades, I was the only one who was a three-star recruit, everyone else on the list had 5 or 4 stars next to their names.

SENIOR HIGH SCHOOL SEASON

Still working out on the east side that offseason, but this year I switched it up just like big bro did going into his senior year. I made a call to Howard Ware and started working out with him. All summer I lifted weights early in the a.m. with Coach Ware and in the afternoons I headed to Yellow Jacket Stadium and ran with the Austin Striders Track Club. I was all business coming into my senior year. I ended up having an amazing senior season to say the least. Still have a record at my high school for a 99-yard touchdown run. A record that would never ever be broken, it can only be tied. Against all odds I finally left my stamp at that school.

The phone rings even less the whole year, despite having a better season. There's one game against Bowie where I had 265 yards by the third quarter and I sat out the whole fourth quarter. In another game I had 263 yards versus Akins and sat out the whole fourth quarter. I would have set more records for my high school, probably still standing to this day, but coach was like, "Tyler, you take a seat." So my numbers are still matriculating. My performance on the field had gotten better. My speed had increased. I put my head down and worked. My academics were even better. I started working on my personal academic goals myself. This is how I knew I was dope. This is where I started to figure out like, "Yo, you are actually very smart Tyler Campbell."

UNSIGNED

I'll never forget that feeling I had when I realized I wasn't getting recruited. It felt like a scene out of the Twilight Zone. I didn't sign a letter of intent my senior year. Everyone kept asking, "Why not? What happened? You're one of the top running backs in the state." My only response would be," I don't know." Often, I had no words or answers just blank stares.

A few months prior to signing day, I called San Diego State University because that's the school I always wanted to go to at my core. Even more than Notre Dame. SDSU had offered me a scholarship prior to everything that had transpired and it was in California. I'd never been to Cali like that. It was only 15 minutes from the beach, plenty of palm trees and sunshine. The school colors were dope: red and black, just like the colors worn by my favorite player from the Atlanta Falcons, Michael Vick. I picked up the phone in the study of our house. I was looking directly at this huge picture of my dad's favorite country music singer, Willie Nelson. I silently said to myself, "today is going to be a great day." I started dialing the number of the running back coach at San Diego State named Wally Gaskins. He answered and I said, "Coach, this is Tyler Campbell and I am ready to be an Aztec" but to my surprise, he said, "Tyler we thought you were committed to Texas A&M so you no longer have a scholarship here." Just like that dreams of being Aztec were left blowing in the wind.

Next I reached out to Baylor University. It wasn't my favorite school, but it was a scholarship and I promised my parents that they would not have to pay for my education. I called the coach and told him I want to be a Baylor Bear. The coach was geeked, but he said, "Tyler this is a big decision. Let me come down for an in-home visit and make sure you are completely comfortable before you commit." It was a great visit and as I walked him to the door I said, "Coach, can I have a few days to make sure this is what I want?" He kindly replied, "Tyler take all the time you need." A few days went by and I decided to commit to Baylor so my promise would be upheld to my family. I called the coach in the parking lot at Westlake. He picked up the phone and I said, "Coach I am ready to be a Bear." To my shock and surprise he replied, "Tyler, we had a running back commit yesterday. You can't come to our school." It felt like all air had left my body and I became filled with emotions of embarrassment and anger. My scholarships are all gone. Nowhere to go play, I'd **lost the ball** it seemed.

Signing day was that February, I did not sign a letter of intent. Highs and lows again. I couldn't wrap my mind around the fact that I'd had my best football season ever, and none of the colleges that recruited me wanted to take a chance on me. Record setting but not good enough. Signing day is a big deal, especially in the state of Texas. My name was not in any newspapers that next day. Nothing. Silence. Crickets. My parents tried to be as supportive as they could but I also knew they were like, 'this is something he's got to go through. This is something he's going to have to figure out.' I felt alone. See, I knew I could play ball, but didn't know where or how I was going to get there. I told my parents that they wouldn't have to pay for school for me. Now I had no school that even wanted me. I did not attend any college camps that off season leading up to my senior year because I was trying to get myself together mentally. Just wanted to focus on starting clean and making better decisions with my life. By the end of my recruiting process, I had been downgraded to a two-star recruit. "Lord, let Your will be done", I said to myself regardless of the odds. With no school recruiters in site, here I am applying to schools now. I never filled out college applications and this was truly a learning experience for me. I really struggled with it mentally. I filled out one to University of Houston and I filled out one to University of Arizona. I heard they had good business schools. I got accepted into both. Academically I was prepared, but I didn't want to attend them. I told my mom and pop, "I don't want this. Mom, I can play ball. I really can. I know I can. I just need someone to give me a chance."

Now it's April, graduation's coming and I still don't have a place to go to school. A coach by the name of John Paradez comes to Westlake and he lays a card on my head coach's desk. Coach Long knew how badly I wanted to play ball and so he gave me the card during a passing period in the hallway. It read, 'Pasadena City College' (PCC), a junior college (JC) in Pasadena, California. There were junior colleges in Texas that offered scholarships, dorms, everything, the whole nine. It wasn't like playing football at a junior college was unheard of. Cam Newton came back and went to Blinn Junior College before bouncing back. Junior college in Texas is good because it's still all about football.

California Junior College offered no scholarships. If I went out west, I was going to be out there on my own. Why? Because financially I didn't qualify for financial aid. I didn't have that option of receiving assistance. I come from too much of an affluent family. Remember, I told my family they wouldn't have to pay for my education. Through my eyes that also included room and board. Heartbroken, I asked my mom if I could go and she said, "Yeah, you can go. Tyler, you can go." She said, "Let's take a plane trip out there." We booked a trip with Southwest Airlines. We flew into Bob Hope Airport in Burbank, CA and as soon as we got off the plane I saw palm trees. I was ecstatic and feeling that California love right away. I'll never forget going to Pasadena City College. I saw a bust of Jackie Robinson there. I saw filmmaker John Singleton's name in the library. He wrote the 1991 classic, 'Boyz N The Hood'. The experience was too much to capture in words. The people who had come through Pasadena City College were epic. This place was special. I recall being in awe of Jackie Robinson's bust. You see, everybody likes to talk about the UCLA Jackie, but people forget that he that he went to Pasadena City College first.

I said, "Man, Jackie Robinson came here and made something of himself. John Singleton came here and made something of himself and now the world knows their names. Why can't I do the same thing?" Everyone back home was laughing. They would say, "You going to a junior college?" It was the sobering reminder, that whatever positives come in your life, be excited about them. No matter what, throw your own party. The world is going to try and tear your accomplishments apart. Be reminded that this is your joy and if you're not careful, you'll let the world shred your dreams before you even get them started.

I remember being so excited telling friends or associates about my college journey, and they'd be like, "Man, you're going to a JC." But I remember telling my mom when we got back on the plane. I said, "Mom, I'm going to come here to Pasadena City College. I'm going to make it out." She sternly replied, "That's cool, Tyler. But when you go, you're not coming back home unless you got a degree." I said, "What?" Mom said, "You're not coming home unless you get a degree. If this is your dream, I'll support you wholeheartedly. But you come here, you figure it out and you let this catapult you to walk across the stage with a four-year degree. Not a two-year degree, a four-year degree." I agreed to that. It was my first gigantic decision in life. I chose a college and I could not be more at peace.

Pop had a bus back then, so his driver, Mr. Archie, drove my mother, my grandfather L. G. Smith and myself to the west coast. Final destination being 76 South Bonnie in Pasadena, California. Just off of East Colorado Boulevard and right across the from PCC. Colorado Boulevard was same street that the famous Rose Parade comes down every year on TV.

PCC was a unique situation at the time, a lot of kids from the south had also come to play ball at this JC that year. All my roommates were from the New Orleans area except Big Cliff and Paulo. Cliff was from Colorado. Paulo, was a Samoan from Hawaii. It was my first time meeting a Samoan. To be truthful, Paulo is the real reason my mom allowed me come to PCC. He won her trust over with the quickness back when I visited. On the real, Paulo was so chill and dude could sing his tale off. I tell people all the time there is so much more to a football player than a warrior that constantly trains for battle. Paulo was proof.

He could sing just like Bobby Valentino. I would always ask him to sing Bobby's smash hit at the time called, 'Slow Down'. Also rooming with me at 76 South Bonnie were Waheed and Dewayne. Waheed was from Kenner, LA just outside of New Orleans. He was an Egyptian Muslim. I'll never forget walking into his room and seeing a Hookah for the first time. There was so much culture, so much life. It was something my soul had been yearning for. I felt at home. So, I get to Pasadena and I'm rocking on this journey of self-discovery. I remember in that moment feeling like, Cali just got a different vibe all together. I was seeing cats with Chuck Taylors, throwing up Bs and Cs (hand signs for 'bloods' and crips'). There were so many color restrictions as a black male that I had to learn with the quickness. It was like if we go here, don't wear red. If you wore blue over on that side of the city, you're in trouble. A new nickname came to the forefront as my teammates began calling me "TC." Tyler lived in Texas, but TC was carving out his own journey on the west coast. I was 'doing me' and it felt great.

During my time in Pasadena I met a lot of great people. I forged a lot of lasting relationships and a brotherhood with several that is still in tack to this day. I'm immersed in this new culture at every direction I turn. One of my newfound friends from the N.O. (short for New Orleans) ended up being my ace in the hole. His name was Jumal. Jumal used to tell me stories about growing up in the N.O. and how he had to witness his cousin get shot and killed right before his eyes in his early years. Just an example of the intimate conversation that only brothers could share. Jumal explained how tragic real life experiences messed him up psychologically. He later expressed that the hood wasn't always that bad. It's just the bad stories are what the media likes to focus on. He schooled me on some of the hidden treasures and life lessons he had acquired from growing up in the N.O. Also, in the same apartment complex was Antoine, who was originally from the Magnolia projects. He was always telling me, "TC, home ain't all that bad, but it's not all that great either. There are some bright spots and things that we experienced in the hood too just like Jumal mentioned." They used to take me underneath their wings because I was young, 17 at the time, and I was green from suburbia life. Jumal was the one who looked out for me the most. He had his own nickname for me that he still uses to this day 'T-Town'. He would say, "T-Town, be careful what you say out cher, ya heard me." Cats knew that I was from the burbs. So they were like, "Man, don't wear that. Mm-mm (negative). Don't put them clothes on. Don't put them shoes on bro. Don't play that music. You know what I'm saying?" It was like cats knew that there was opportunity in me. They really just wanted to see me make it out of JC. That was the ultimate goal for all of us, but at the end of the day it was always all love at PCC. More love than I ever felt anywhere else and we were all coming from a stream of brokenness. Everybody was either a dope athlete that fell through the cracks, didn't have the grades or you came from a volatile situation. You had a team full of individuals that had to learn how to survive just to play the game.

Some cats on the team would do their best not to say words that started with a 'C'. For example, instead of saying Compton they would say 'Bompton'. It was new to me but I was quickly learning that it was just a part of the culture in the area I was in. I know it sounds crazy but I still felt free at PCC and right at home. I was building relationships with a new band of brothers on the team. Our apartment was right next to the 99 Cent store, which was a blessing because you could really stretch your money there. Some of us were working and doing whatever we could to keep a dream alive. There was so much brokenness but I promise, at the heart of 76 South Bonnie, there was always love. We would put all our money together and Jumal would cook. Even his canned peas and carrots were on point. He also knew how to make gumbo. Mal was always like, "Man, I can cook it for you. You all just got to chip in for the groceries." He was a jack of all trades. If you needed a haircut or crispy lineup, Mal would breakout his clippers and hook you up with a fresh fade in the kitchen. My hair, at this time in my life, was something I began to love and embrace. I had been growing it out for months prior and never left home without afro pic in pocket.

As I mentioned before, my mother wouldn't allow braids in her house. Now I have independency and I could rock a hairstyle I had been longing for. I'll never forget how much joy and happiness there was in my heart the first time I got my hair braided. My teammate Mike, from Monrovia, had a friend who I nicknamed Shorty because of her stature. Shorty would come do my hair in our apartment. There was a peace that I would experience when getting my hair done by her. A process and conversation I always enjoyed. She was taking my afro and producing an amazing work of art with grace. You see getting my hair done just felt as if I was getting closer to my roots in a way that I had never experienced growing up on the west side of Austin. After I developed a little hang time with my braids, Mal was like, "Yo, T-Town, put some shells back there." Shorty didn't know how to do it, but Mal pulled out some shells and put them in for me. I am telling you, he was a big brother for real, to me. My blackness, my genuine love for my people was really starting to flow in the most memorable way. Keeping it all the way 100, things were deeply broken around us at Pasadena City College. I think we won two games total for the year but believe me when I tell you it was also home to some of the best times in my life.

After earning a starting position at Fullback coming out of camp, I ended up getting hurt the second quarter of the second game of the season. A shoulder injury that sidelined me for the entire year. What made it worse was that my mom had caught a flight out to watch me play that same game. It reminded me emotionally of that same, hopeless feeling I felt when I was in alternative school. I didn't even want to get out of bed to go to class. I felt like it's time to throw in the towel, ball just isn't for me. I'll never forget my phone ringing unexpectedly one early morning. It was my father calling to console and comfort his baby boy. Simply put, he said, "You are a Campbell, Tyler, and a Campbell never quits. You see, if you never quit, you can never lose. No one told you it was going to be easy, you have to fight and pay attention to what the Lord is trying to teach you."

I had to look at life through a different lens with ball gone. I loved my teammates so much and what I noticed, contrary to the outside world's beliefs, was they weren't in JC because they didn't have the smarts. So many were just dealt a bad hand in life. These men were brilliant individuals. Their defense mechanisms were so powerful. They could feel danger. These men could smell trouble. My friends could sense a threat. They knew when they were talking to somebody who didn't have their best interests at heart. They knew it because of what they have been through in their lives thus far. There were life lessons from my teammates all around me and I needed to wake up and pay attention off the field.

I used to take Jumal to the library with me. He had never been in the library before. The things I took for granted were new experiences for him. Once I showed him where the library was and how to study, and then Mal turned his grades upside down. It was like I saw brilliance up close and personal. I used to say to myself while starring at the ceiling listening to burned R&B cd's, "I wish the world of doubters could just see the brilliance of our people instead of judging or casting stones. They would see so many magnificent, amazing and beautiful people." In the famous words of the Georgia Rap duo Field Mob, "We are all God's property not just Kirk Franklin."

As the semester continued Paulo dropped football and moved out. We all missed him; when Paulo left, a big piece of our home went with him. Our new roommate was Kahlil from New Jersey. It seemed like all of my friends had their own version of saying 'Hi'. For Kahlil it was "Yo, What up, B? What up, son? Everyday B, Everyday." Kahlil brought every bit of east coast flare with him into our home. Dudes from Cali were like, "Wasup Homie." D-Mo from Atlanta would say, "Whas happenin', Shawty " in a thick country accent. Brandon, a.k.a. D-12, from Detroit would salute you with "What Up Tho." Last but not least my New Orleans family would say "Wasup Whodie" like clockwork. I saw so much creative brilliance in my people. I wanted others in the world to see it too. Mal was the eye opener. I didn't really think I was teaching him that much. I was learning so much from him. The least I could do was give him a few tips on how to study that I learned back in high school. As a result, he started doing really well in class and was going to make it out of PCC academically. Now that he had the study tools he was confident he would be ready when colleges came calling.

Anyone that studies or who has played the game of football can tell you that for an offensive player there is nothing worse than fumbling or losing the ball to the opposing team. One bad decision had caused me to lose all of my football scholarships. Literally and figuratively, I had **lost the ball**.

Junior College was a mixed bag for me. There were both moments of happiness and hard times. In the midst of dropping that ball in terms of manhood, the saving grace was, I figured out that I didn't need anyone else to motivate me. I realized that I was enough. I learned that I didn't need to depend on another man, I didn't lean on a teacher, a coach or a friend to be about my work. A 'Campbell never quits' was the phrase I kept on my brain. It's something when you wake up to the greatness of you. I'd began to truly discover that I did not need to have somebody to look over my shoulder, or to push me to class. These were the things that when football was stripped, the ball was dropped. I found myself in this journey and in the process of self-discovery, all things, God-given things named above, were given back to me.

There was a voice in my head that seemed to flick the switch that turned the light of self-sufficiency on in my life. You ever have a moment when something clicks for you? At this point in time in my life I was going through a metamorphosis and pressed reset on my own life. For example, it meant a lot for me to never miss a class. Tapping into my own genius, I started to see that academically, I could be a straight A student with no problem. School became so simple to me as I mastered every course.

In hindsight, I believe it was always a part of my fabric to be a high achiever and it began to come into fruition back when I was placed in the Alternative High School System. My junior year of high school, instead of falling behind, I got ahead. When I was reacclimated, I was relearning stuff all over again because of my focus in the alternative program. It's unbelievable how what you think is breaking you is actually having an opposite effect on your life. Would you believe me if I told you that I found a love for literature again inside of an alternative system? I used to read J. R. Tolkien's novels and get lost in the fact that this dude invented his own freaking language. I'd read all the 'Lord Of The Rings' series during a time period when the movie recreations were smashing box office records in theaters. I had so much time in alternative school. I researched Tolkien and learned that he invented his own languages for the characters in his books. Truly a fascinating gift as a writer, his brilliance drew me in. Tolkien wrote a magnificent trilogy in 'The Lord of The Rings' and it seemed that these movies were the only things people were talking about. I was so hyped at that time. I'm letting everybody know the stuff left out of the movie that was in his books. I would say "You all ain't read the book?" "Oh, the book's too long," they would say. My response was, "What do you mean it's too long?" I found an author to cling to and I was falling in love with words.

At alternative school I would finish my work ahead of time, interestingly enough; when I was with the regular student body, I would struggle to complete it. I'd spend the rest of the day reading J. R. Tolkien books. My momma wouldn't let me go anywhere, so when I was back home, all I could do was read some more. I had discovered a man who was so incredibly creative, that he could invent his own languages for his novels. That was simply mind- blowing for me. It got me thinking about what I could do if I unlocked my fullest potential. Daily, my mind started to soar like, "Tyler, what could your brain upstairs really and truly do?" When taking a trip down memory lane, to me as that 12-year-old kid, there's one thing that changed my life and propelled me forward. That was when I met a lady by the name of Mrs. Schoch. She came from El Paso, TX, so she was used to dealing with minority kids. Mrs. Schoch taught me the importance of sentence structure and planted seeds deep within the soul of my mind that I couldn't fully harvest until years later. Most students thought she was a major pain in the you know what, but really she was like, "You all don't know how blessed you are and I want ya'll to understand. I come from El Paso, an area full of kids and families with some serious hardships in life, that would give to have the resources you have."

Mrs. Schoch got to know my momma and they instantly connected. She is responsible for teaching me that my words could set me free. She instilled in me that there is power in understanding grammar and sentence structure. Things like predicate nominatives, predicate adjectives, appositives, subject, verb agreements, infinitives and prepositional phrases. I fell head over heels in love actually with how sentences were put together. Thanks to Mrs. Schoch and the hidden gems she poured into me I would later discover and appraise the value of my own jewels.

When I was in Junior College, I did a winter session because I knew it was going to put me that much more ahead academically than my counterparts. Separating myself from the pack, I stayed behind to study. Everyone else went home for the break. I went home for a week for Christmas and I came right back to Pasadena. Academically, there was a yearning to really execute in the classroom, the same way football was for me. For the first time in my life I was making moves without the football. Just like on the football field it was my goal to break every tackle. Now there was the same drive academically, compounded by a fearless work ethic. There were times I didn't even need an alarm clock to get up at 4 a.m., and go run on the track at PCC in the pitch black. It was becoming second nature to put in the extra work. All during the spring semester I would work out on my own in the a.m. and then come back in the afternoon and train with my teammates. I was getting my body ready for an impactful season with no injuries.

As much as it looked like I'd done a 180 degree turnaround, it's like God was prepping me to make sure my mind was ready to receive His hand-off for greater things. God was simply taking me through Faith Class 101. He stripped me of something to gain. He took football away for a moment for the greater good. I could now see myself clearly because of the Greater One living inside of me. It felt like God was testing me until I mastered His call. God gave me some questions and had birth answers inside of me at the same time. Can you focus on your academics? Yes. Can you still be a leader amongst men? Yes. Tyler, can you still work for what you want, even when you can't see the finish line? My answer was certainly yes.

When that day I got the ball back showed up for me, it occurred because I was being obedient to the Man up above. I was submitting to the path of what He was trying to make up for me as a man. Those were his orders if I wanted to receive the blessing He had behind closed doors for me. You see, the moment for that to work started when I hurt my shoulder in the second game of the season. It was the means to a new beginning in my life. I understood that I must keep walking and talking in faith. It was imperative that I read my Bible every day without fail. Jumal and I grew closer to the Lord. We surfed the bible together and went to church, while other teammates were still sleeping from the night before.

Even when football season wasn't going, we went to another level spiritually. I had a black male, accountability partner who loved the Lord like I did and we were trying to navigate through life together. I saw God work in my life. I saw that being obedient, would allow me to walk with confidence for this next journey. I don't know what it's going to look like, I know it's probably going to be some hell in here. I know it's going to be some trying times and hurtful times off in this thing, but I know my Man's going to deliver me. Somehow, someway, He will deliver me. I kept telling myself, "This is going to work out as long as I do not quit, and I don't lose sight of Him. It's all on you, TC, sink or swim, the choice is yours."

SAN DIEGO STATE

I always say that it was big for me at the age of 16 to tell my mother and my father that they didn't t have to worry about me academically because I would get a full scholarship. I got a rebirth of that conversation when Andy Buh, the linebacker's coach at San Diego State University, came on the random to PCC. He showed up to 7 on 7 drills that summer before the start of the season. I didn't know who he was but I saw the logo on his shirt that said S.D.S.U. If there was ever a weakness about my game, it was that I had terrible catching skills. The crazy thing was on that day I didn't drop a single pass and scored multiple touchdowns. A week later I received a phone call with a full ride scholarship offer to San Diego State University. I cried tears of joy after the call, lifted my hands to the sky and said "thank you, Jesus." When that letter of intent officially came in the mail, I called my mother and said, "You don't have to worry about me anymore momma." I finally got the chance to have that conversation again. I was going to be an Aztec. God allowing me to touch that dream, getting to that campus, it meant something different to me.

The air riding down the 5 Freeway was so crisp. The drive was beautiful, first LA, then Orange County and then Laguna. All were such beautiful places and at times during the drive you would be right alongside the Ocean. The hidden imagery was that the same people who dropped me off at PCC after graduating high school, were the ones accompanying on my transition to SDSU. My Paw Paw L.G., mom and Mr. Archie fired up the bus once again from Texas. I felt like we were all winning on that special day. I felt like we were all celebrating. I felt my mother's excitement even when she wasn't talking. She told her baby son, "Don't come back without that degree." I went to the winter school sessions and I had put my time in. Now here we are riding alongside each other to San Diego State, the school I always thought so highly of since I was 16. It was like a dream or a fairy tale. I kept waiting for someone to pinch me to wake me up. Even though my dad couldn't physically be there because of an injury, I carried that conversation of 'A Campbell Never Quits' and that if I quit at one thing I would quit at everything for the rest of my life. I understood that it was on his shoulders that I stand. I could feel his presence, man, what an incredible, indescribable feeling. Now here I am, making the transition from PCC to SDSU. I always heard older folks singing a song in church that said, "The Lord may not come when you want Him, but He'll be there right on time. He's an on-time God, yes he is." The journey had been tough and lonely, but the Lord just showed up right on time. I grew closer to Him because I witnessed the miracle he just created in my life. Now a new journey was on the horizon at SDSU.

I was stepping into an added level of manhood, but that was created because I was obedient to The Trinity. I was ready to make that leap now. You see, I understood I wasn't ready to make the leap to a 4-year university straight out of high school. That's why I had to go to junior college. I just wasn't ready or positioned where He needed for me to be.

After **losing that ball**, the beautiful thing about it is, two things happen: Either the opposing team is going to get that thing and take advantage of your mishap, your unawareness, your mistake, or you would have the opportunity to fall back on it and recover it. Better yet, take it from where it is that you left off and turn it into something. I had dropped it, but on now I am heading down the I-5 South toward I-8 East, exiting Fairmount Avenue and pushing up Montezuma Rd. It's like, I don't know. I was taking the ball and it was going somewhere. I don't think I had flashed a smile this wide in a long, long time.

I'd be remised if I didn't tell this part of the story. Remember back in high school when I fumbled the ball forfeiting my scholarships by the poor decisions I made in high school? Life was looking to create a theatrical ending, similar to that of JR Tolkien's Novels, it just needed to find the right person to play the leading role. You see my scholarship to SDSU, this is a second go round, which became available because an incoming Freshman lost his opportunity due to misconduct off the field. Truly it was a case of all things working together for good and things coming full circle.

LeCharls McDaniel was the running back coach on The Mesa. He was like another father figure. He had played in the league himself and even won a Super Bowl Ring during his time with the Washington Redskins. He took pride in being that father figure for black kids on the football team, whether you were wide receiver, lineman, DB, whatever, it didn't matter. He understood the monumental leaps as young men that we can make for our families with furthering our education and excelling on the field. He knew what kids thought, so he loved everyone in a different way. Coach Mac possessed a special gift for communicating with people. He knew that if he's too hard on some cats, he'll drive them to quitting because of what that young man has been through in life. That's powerful, that's awareness, the man knew his kids.

Training camp was on the horizon and because I received my scholarship only a few weeks prior, they didn't really have a place for me. I put all my baggage in a coach's closet because it was so last minute. My academic advisor, Bre, hit it off with my mother immediately. My mama felt comfortable, how she felt about PCC after she spoke to Paulo. Mom didn't care about coaches. She had been around the game for decades because of pop, she understood the game and wasn't even trippin' on it. Just like any other mother her focus was all on academics.

Sometimes all that glitters isn't gold, something had happened with the Clearing House and my transcripts from PCC. For some reason they weren't getting cleared. I had great grades. They just didn't transfer over to State like they were supposed to. All my stuff got put on hold just like my bags in the coach's office. I mean, everything was put on hold, it was completely out of my control. "Alright we got to get back to Texas. You're here at State. We know you're not here right now but it's eventually going to happen.", is what my grandfather and mother told me; at that moment, I realized I was on my own. It was bittersweet saying 'good bye', especially since I could not participate when camp started.

Every newcomer had to address the team in meeting room on the first day of check-ins. That meant standing up in front of everybody and introducing yourself. I know Cats did their homework, and I know what the homework is on me. This is Earl Campbell's son. Let's see what he is about. It's like Pasadena all over again. I remember getting up there and I said, "My name is Tyler Campbell, but I go by TC. I'm coming by way of Pasadena City College, but I'm from the great State of Texas."

The only problem was that I couldn't let football intervene for me when I needed it to. I checked in and they gave me jersey number 23. I've been 32, and now it's flipped. I'm a little in my feelings, but I understood the number doesn't make the player, the player makes the number. I was Ginuwine, "So Anxious" to get out there and show my stuff. Instead, I had to sit in the coach's office while everybody was practicing. It was torture being so close but yet so far from playing the game I loved. I wasn't even allowed to be in the dorms because I wasn't technically admitted into the school.

It was this way for a week. They had to find me a place to stay. I wasn't allowed to be in the dorm. It was as if I were a ghost. I had to stay with "Mr. Abs On The Way", a.k.a. J-Shaw. Dude loved playing Madden. What was dope was that he found a place for us to workout at so we could stay in shape for camp. I was serious with it. You know you can feel people watching you when you are in the gym? Shaw knew for me it wasn't just going to be no regular workout.

He told me that he was from Palmdale, California. I knew where Palmdale was because we had gotten blown out by College of The Canyons, my first game at PCC which wasn't too far from there. So we had a conversation, but I already knew my mental approach towards the game. That's not where he was at that time. A few days had passed and I finally got the call, " TC, come on in, you have been cleared." I got in and got the helmet on. Now, I had to start all over. Everybody else was in full pads. I had to follow the protocol and gradually work myself up to full pads which took another 3 or 4 days. Finally, I got the chance to blend in with everyone else and wear full pads. I remember Coach Mac, saying "You're behind, but we need to see what you can do really quickly." UCLA was our first

TYLER CAMPBELL

game. They had Maurice Jones-Drew and Marcedes Lewis. It was going to be a dog fight. UCLA vs San Diego State, that's a big game to be precise, the one that we had never won up to this point in 2005. Even NFL Hall of Famer, Marshall Faulk, couldn't lead the Aztecs over the Bruins in the nineties. We felt that this year was going to be different for us.

That morning 2-A Day practice, Coach Mac put me in with the 1st team's offense. It was 1's vs 1's. I'll never forget it. We had JB, Freddy (who went on to win a Super Bowl with the Indianapolis Colts) and Antwan (who later played for the San Diego Chargers and San Francisco 49ers). I knew them because I studied the roster book when I couldn't get admitted into school. My first time in the huddle and Coach Tom Kraft, our head coach, called a run. It was 300, a zone play. That meant it starts to the left and by my third step, I should have the ball from our QB Kevin (Now Offensive Coordinator in the NFL). Prior to the play, I get in my stance and scan the field to get a read on the defense pre-snap. Then the ball was snapped. I read my keys. I know the linebackers are going to fill their gaps with authority. So I must press the hole to get them to sell out to their right to open up a cutback lane to my right. I knew how it would go before the play even started.

I didn't know the playbook that well. I had only been in practice a few days. I was thrown in there cold turkey. It didn't matter, one thing you never forget is how to 'tote the rock'. My instincts kicked in immediately. I took my keys, left step, a right step, by the time you hit your third step you should be downhill to press the hole. I got the ball and now I'm pressing. I see all the linebackers over committing, just like in my pre snap vision, to the left side of offensive line of scrimmage. I recognize it and after the press I cut back right to the opposite to hole. It worked like magic.

All I saw was daylight. I get to the next level passing the

linebackers. Now, you are in running-back heaven. What I mean by this is, there is no view sweeter than reaching the last level of the defense and with a 1 on 1 matchup with a safety. I believe his name was Matt. I know Matt's coming down hill to save the day. In that moment, I know that's time to make a statement. Coach Mac said I had to show him what I had and earn the respect of my teammates. I wanted to reward the offensive line by finishing what they started. I remember lowering my left shoulder and curling the ball in the right arm. Matt came down as hard as he could from the safety spot, and I gave him all of my lowered left shoulder and ran him over. I could hear, "Oooooooh", because everybody's on the sideline, to the right. That's my first carry at SDSU. In that moment I knew that I could play Division 1 college football. It was the same game I've been playing since the 7th grade.

The next play after that was a pass. Then we ran the same run play as the first but to the opposite side. I press the hole again, but this time the defense was ready. They got penetration and my ankle got rolled on in the pile. It just seemed like my life was always on a roller coaster. I had the high of that 1st play and before I could blink my legs were pulled out from underneath me. "Why?" I kept saying to myself. I felt something pop within the ankle. I finished the rest of practice on a limp. It was a two-a-day practice. I got ice after practice, but I had no push off whatsoever and my ankle was swollen. Why did everything have to always be a fight?

I remember being in the cafeteria after that first practice of the day. My ankle was throbbing, but there was no time to complain because the real show was coming. Camp Tradition was that every newcomer had to sing a song in front of the team and today it was my turn. I'm riding this wave of momentum as people were still talking about that one run I had. I stood on-top of chair and went old school. The Five Heartbeats, to be specific. I opened my mouth with authority and totally butchered the song 'Nights Like This'.

Thankfully it was a song the brothas on the team knew along with some of the coaches. People started clapping and singing along, it was all love, but thank God I never had to sing ever again.

And so, I was winning and finding my place on the team. It was time for me to grow up. You discovered yourself, but now God intervened to give you that second chance. So with that second chance, all business, all gas, no brakes. Straight business only.

That was the beginning of me discovering my best friend from S.D.S.U. His name was Matt and he played tight end. He sat down with me that day in the cafeteria. I learned he was from Colorado and was real chill. I was elated because I had found someone who approached the game just like me. Matt was all business, meaning he ate, slept, walked and talked football. It was the beginning of a friendship that exists to this day. Speaking of friendships, there was one running back from New Orleans on the team. His name was Michael. He was an upper classman, a senior. Yo, I loved Mike and we spoke the same language. TC, "Big fella you gotta approach practice like this and be responsible off the field like this", I can hear him talking in that thick accent I took for granted hearing from my old teammates at PCC. The ability to meet someone from New Orleans was further confirmation that I made the right decision coming to SDSU. Mike was a mentor who took me under his wing. A standup man on and off the field, ya heard me.

I ended up redshirting my first year on campus. Coach Mac gave me a choice. He said, "Would you like to play, or would you red shirt?" I thought I was so behind on the playbook that I took the safe route and asked for the redshirt. It was a big mistake on my end, one that I still regret to this day. I should have just gone with it and had enough confidence in myself to know that I would pick it up as the season progressed. My ankle was a problem but everybody plays hurt in this game.

Accept pain and accept hurt, and just put all that stuff deep down inside. That's what I did. That's what Sophmore year was all about. You're not playing football. I stayed in the freshman dorms a lot of times on the weekends and everybody else would be out partying, living it up with their first year of independency. I had already experienced that. The party scene wasn't for me; I had been through so much to get to this point. I had been given a second chance and I was so fearful of blowing it. I didn't want to put myself in a situation where a poor decision landed me back home in Austin.

San Diego State was one of the top party schools in the country at that time. As I look back on those times, I often wonder was it fear or did I just understand the meaning of sacrifice that made me act that way. Maybe I was just an 18-year-old young man fighting battles internally and learning how to navigate life. Either way it was just further confirmation that this year would be one filled with growing pains.

I remember being at the Athletic Center on my first day of school, and this girl comes up to me in the in the computer lab. There's one printer in there, so all your printouts go to this one spot. Back then I always wore a silver mirror image necklace. You know those necklaces you could get made at the kiosk places in the mall. The photo in the necklace was of me with my girlfriend from high school. This girl comes up to me and her name was Shana. As a matter of fact, she's the first girl I ever had a conversation with at San Diego State. Shana came up to me, and was like, "What you got on that necklace? Let me see," something like that. Right off the bat, I was in defense mode because my necklace was my business and it didn't concern her. I have me and this girl on this thing and I know that image bothered her. She looked at the necklace, and said, something like, "Is this your girl?" We butt heads for quite a while after that first encounter. So not only was football not going according to the plan, but I was struggling off the field to fit in. I missed 76 South Bonnie Ave.

My first year at State I was an emotional mess internally that I could keep hidden from the world outwardly. A coping mechanism I learned to develop at a very early age. I am thankful for the deliverance and the blessing to get to State, but I also want to be transparent and say there were some low moments. Please buckle in, I want you to get a window seat into my heart. At that particular time my relationship with my girlfriend was on the rocks in a big way. Although she never admitted it, I felt she wasn't as committed to the relationship as I was. That wasn't the worst part though. I promised you a window seat so here it is. The sad part was as a young man I thought so low of myself that I believed I wasn't deserving of better, that this was payback for me breaking up with her after high school. I didn't understand my worth or stand behind my words with confidence. I didn't believe that I deserved to have somebody or think that there was somebody out there who could love me and see me and cherish me for just me.

As a result, I got to a level of acceptance. I knew that things weren't great. I knew our relationship wasn't in a great place. Sadly, I accepted those things and felt like, okay, Tyler, this is what long distance relationships are. You are going to have to wait, be silent and weather the storm. "Pray for things to get better," I kept telling myself. I failed to recognize that the answer to the prayer was stepping outside my comfort zone of acceptance. I knew what I wanted, but I couldn't put it into action. I was scared of the unknown. The Lord was asking me to leap, but I was too fearful of making the jump. This moment in my life is where tough lessons off the field were being taught and I was failing the class. There were other people out there for me to meet, but I wouldn't take the steps because I couldn't see the staircase. I desperately yearned for someone to love me for me at my core. In so many ways I was still that fearful 12-year-old emotionally torn and unconfident boy that was in his own head.

CHAPTER 4 "Offsides"

One of the most important and initial first lessons drilled into my head as a kid playing football was to never, ever jump **offsides**. In other words, you don't step across the line of scrimmage until the ball is snapped. If you do you cause a penalty to occur, which results in moving the ball in the opposite direction of your opponent's end zone. Rule number one: don't keep your eyes on the players but fixate them on the ball to avoid finding yourself offsides.

Challenging years for me were the last three years of college at San Diego State. It seemed there was a pattern forming almost like parts to a jigsaw puzzle, with common edge pieces of my life labeled highs and lows. Just when I was finding my rhythm, we get an entirely new coaching staff. I got switched to fullback again after playing the running back position. I made up in my mind to make the best out of any and all opportunities that were given to me.

I've learned that oftentimes, you just need a little light to bring hope inside of a tunnel. Light shines on common faces onto familiar faces. A good friend, solid dude and fellow running back Atiyyah ended up becoming an All-Conference Player. I played fullback and special teams. I wanted to be a regular guy who had a dream of becoming great. At the time, I was a very unhappy guy to be precise, but I was not going to show it. I instead choose to hold it all in. On the outside, I was calm, cool, and collective but on the inside, I'm drowning amidst my own private storm. I was always someone who was trying to help others see that we all could be different. Honestly, I did not want the label to stick on us that we fit the status quo of being jocks. There's more to us than sports.

I continued to soar as a man and as a teammate over the next couple of years, in terms of leadership, and being present for my peers. Playing my role was far bigger than the stats and jersey on game day. I was becoming more comfortable in my own skin. There were sparks of self-love immerging and I was beginning to love Tyler Campbell. My friend, loving yourself is contagious and those around you can feel and see it. On our team, there was a Captain's Council for each grade level and every time, I was always one of the captains for my class. This position required you to sit and talk with Coach about what is going on with the team. It was truly an honor to hold this position.

"A man's gift [given in love or courtesy] makes room for him and brings him before great men."— Proverbs 18:16 - Amplified Version

My faith continued to blossom like the palm trees in my view. I'm reading Proverbs on the regular and gaining wisdom and food for my soul daily. I learned to memorize parts of Proverbs, and would quote them to myself and others habitually.

"Do not let mercy and kindness and truth leave you [instead let these qualities define you]; Bind them [securely] around your neck, Write them on the tablet of your heart. So find favor and high esteem in the sight of God and man."— Proverbs 3:3-4- Amplified Version

My faith kept rolling and kindled a fire within me that until this day can't be quenched. Faith was becoming my backbone and anchor to life's wind and waves.

I am blossoming into my own manhood, and that was how junior year closed. With that said, I ended up becoming the Special Teams

Player of the year for my football team. I received the award with humility and was honored among men. See, I looked at special teams from a view most people didn't. I looked at it as an opportunity to give my team my best, and I did.

The reward of humility [that is, having a realistic view of one's importance] and the [reverent, worshipful] fear of the Lord Is riches, honor, and life."— Proverbs 22:4 - Amplified Version

My first real great season paved the way for me. Also, within the year I played fullback a lot more and was becoming a go-to player. Just blocking for the most part, but still I'm in there. I'm not just a special teams' player, I'm actually playing and with that I'm humble and hungry at the same time. Every time I came in the game, it was either going to be a pass or the other back was going to run it, not me. Nevertheless, I didn't mind blocking for my teammates. These were two skills I initially was terrible at but got more comfortable doing with practice. Ironically (blocking and catching) those are actually things in my game that began to thrive. You're scanning this page right now; I want you to pause to let the previous sentence marinate on your cerebrum. What you are deficient in will become your proficiency. The terrible parts of my game started to grow. I really had built something that Tyler could be proud of in terms of, who I was for my teammates, who I was as a human being.

Beyond football, I'd became a consistent scholar athlete. I graduated early that spring. The following year, I was going to be in the Masters School of Public Administration for my final year of college football. My mother was reeking with pride to say the least. At that time, I'd exceeded my mother and my own expectations. Not only had I made good on the promise to mom, I matriculated college earlier while maintaining a rigorous football schedule. Off the field I'd raised the bar and there are no words that can be confined to the pages of this book that can truly measure how I felt.

I'll never forget the game at Notre Dame, Senior year. After that game, I remember I ended up tackling Golden Tate, when he was receiving the ball. The way I tackled him, it was a mistake, because I wasn't the first one down the field like I was supposed to be on kickoff team as a headhunter. I was actually one of the last ones. But it made for a great tackle. We're on ABC broadcast because it's Notre Dame. I do all my blocking right as a fullback. We should have won the game. My roommate Matt had 9 catches for 60 yards in that football game. This put Matt on the map because 7 of the catches were 3rd down conversions. He and I felt he had literally stamped his ticket to pro football off of that nationally televised game.

I felt as if when I received the ball, great things would happen. My father came to see me against Colorado State. It was a big deal because my dad got on an airplane just to watch me play. That was all love because I knew how badly that hurt my dad's body. His back was so beat up that I knew the slightest turbulence would rack his spine and leave him in agony with every bump. My dad had been through so many back surgeries by now but he pushed himself to watch his son play live from the stands. People couldn't believe that Earl Campbell was out there. Even my own coaches were amazed and didn't know my dad was coming to see me play. I didn't care how his body looked. The image of my father's physical battle serves as trails of greatness that I trace to this very day. Dad is more than just a legendary football player; he is my father first. No one can take away the way my father played that game. I asked him to come because I was starting fullback yes, but I was also 2nd string running back now. The running back room had been decimated by injury. So I knew I would get to carry the rock. It was something I had been waiting 3 years for.

Atiyyah had a good game with over 100 yards. I got less carries, but the ones I did have were monumental because of the yardage per carry. You can't help but to notice that. I remember we were down by six in the fourth quarter. We're driving down the field with just under two minutes left. The pass play was supposed to go to Atiyyah. The route was a flare out of the backfield. The linebacker, if he bites, you go straight up. If he stays where he is, you run a flat. Our quarterback, Ryan, called an audible and flipped the play to the other side. That meant in all likelihood the ball was coming to me. I could feel the vibration against my helmet as my running backs coach was screaming from the sideline because I hadn't caught a pass in a game up to this point in my career. I was always just a blocker. I knew it wasn't the call Coach Holden wanted. I always felt he didn't believe in me for some reason, but I did all the things right. I always felt I should be playing more, but I never complained and always put forth my best effort. Even if that meant tying a rope around my waist and pulling a tire after practice while everyone else went into the locker room. There are always politics in whatever endeavor you choose. I knew better than to let that be an excuse for not giving my best for my team.

Now back to the CSU game, it's on me to read my keys. Either you run the flat, or you hook it into a flare. I'll never forget it, CSU's linebacker number 56 (Ricky Brewer), came up and blitzed. I turned and I got my eyes on him to read. I saw his footsteps, out the corner of my eye, step down, and I knew as soon as he stepped down that was my cue to run forward. The ball seemed like it was in the air for a lifetime, but when it came down I caught it and was flying down the sideline. It was 30 yards or more I picked up. So now we were in the red zone position and threatening to score. The crowd in the stadium was going nuts and wild with excitement. The quarterback runs up to spike the ball. We have a chance to beat Colorado State.

Unfortunately, we ended up losing the game on the next play with an interception but I didn't care. I know you're supposed to win but having my father in the stands was victory enough. The whole camera crew was fixed on my dad throughout the game. I learned that even all the way out in San Diego, CA that that 'Campbell' name means something powerful. That very thing was one of the reasons I came to California to escape. Tonight though it felt different, I felt proud. Can you imagine how I felt inside knowing my dad was there looking at me play live. Talk about history in the making. I was there five years. It was always my mother who came out due to the frailty of my dad's body but this time my pop was in the stands.

That was my first time really seeing how people react to him outside of Texas. My own coaches had nothing to say to Earl Campbell. I believe they were captured by his greatness.

Two weeks later bought on a tall task in BYU. In a freak exchange of events, one our running backs was supposed to return but could not due to injury. That meant I would be playing both positions again just like against CSU. BYU was ranked number 15 in the country. The game was going to be played on the Mountain West Network. We didn't get to play on TV often so this was special. Commentators had called and interviewed me that week so they would have talking material about me for the game. I felt something special was going to happen for me Saturday in Provo, Utah. My first carry came in the first quarter and I took the ball of tackle for a 12 yard carry that ended with a jarring collision with their safety. It was important to send a message at the end of any run so defenders knew they better come correct. I knew it would only get better for me from there if I could be patient. That day we ran a lot of two running back sets, meaning two running backs were in the backfield. The majority of the time the ball was never going to me. I would always still be a blocker even though the plays were designed for two running backs. The only way I was going to get the ball was if our other running back, Atiyyah needed a break. It was a fast paced offense, so once you're in there, you just got to run the plays.

THE BALL CAME OUT

    I didn't know it at the time but there was a big blow up after my 12 yard run from earlier on TV. Those same commentators that interviewed me during the week talked about me for the next 4 minutes of the game. Ya boy was getting some airtime! The commentators were all saying "Earl Campbell's son had a 12 yard run. He's getting his Masters. He's does all this stuff in community. He volunteers for Encanto Elementary School, he really enjoys being there for the kids". I knew nothing about all this going on. I didn't hear about it until I watched the replay of the game. As the game progressed, I got some more carries. I ended up breaking one off for 20 something yards in the second half. This was only my second carry of the game.

    The running back flow, never left me, it was innate. It's like Michael Jordan never losing a jump shot. I never lost the flow of this thing, I've been doing it since I was in eighth grade. I just needed that reminder that I still could because sometimes I felt like I lost it. Let me remind you, my friend, that even though you may have not been able to access that skill you've developed doesn't take away the fact that you can. **Say this with me, "My gift is still there even when it feels unaware".** In that exact moment, I learned that you cannot lose what's deep on the inside.

    The game continued to play out. I'll never forget how I felt at the closure of the game, because we got beat, I mean completely blown out. I realized then that the game meant more me to me than winning. On the plane ride home on Frontier airlines, I always watched Sports Center before takeoff because there were TVs in the headrests. Our game highlights showed up because BYU was in the top 20. At the end of the highlights the stats for the game came up. It read under San Diego State, 'T. Campbell, 4 carries for 43 yards.' Patience prevailed and the Man up above was giving me my roses.

    In my last game against UNLV, my mother and brother came to

see me play. It was senior night and I remember I was running out the tunnel with flowers for my mother. Only when I handed them to her I noticed the petals were all gone because I had hit them with my thigh as I was running towards her. It was too funny. It was senior night and we won the game, what a great way to end my career at State. I scored two touchdowns in that game. In reality, it was just a great way to end my senior year. I even went to the club that night. Every time I showed up at parties, my teammates were hype because they never expected your boy to be there. I was always straight business, football, school and helping my brothers on the team. Overall I was happy at the way I lived my life. I made a commitment to that university when I signed my name on the dotted line. I would ride or die with my teammates on the gridiron, that I would give my academics my best and all that I had to ensure that there was a scholarship left over for somebody else after I was gone. It was a powerful conviction and commitment I had with the team. I stayed with it during my time in college and never wavered.

I never understood how you can make a commitment to something, how you can sign a contract to something, and not hold up your end of the bargain. It was just crazy that that's the way some people thought to me. Again, I felt like that was that peace that I received through my faith walk. I just sensed like, what God got for you, can't nobody steal from you. That's why that senior year was so special, haters couldn't hold me back from getting onto that field and playing the position that I love.

I honestly believe that it was my academics that set the tone for my storybook ending at SDSU in the Spring semester prior. See I put off taking a required freshman speech class until my senior year at State. If you knew me at SDSU before that class, you knew TC didn't speak all that much in crowds of people. I was more standoffish if anything. Perhaps now you can understand why I was so terrified when I walked through the doors of this class for the first time. I'd get butterflies that danced around in the pit of my stomach.

My first speech was on soul food, in Professor Gibson's class. Believe it or not, I did a speech on fatback, collard greens, chitterlings (pig intestines), macaroni and cheese and sweet potatoes. After giving the class a chance, speaking became more comfortable to me than playing football. I wasn't nervous when I got up there and held the classroom hostage with my speech. I got more butterflies playing football after a while. Keeping it 100, my butterflies never went away playing the game. They were always there from the first quarter up until the final whistle. It was so worrisome to me, I felt like I was playing the game scared.

I always wanted to know what it would feel like to play the game of football without butterflies and just be loose. I didn't discover what that feeling was like until I got into this speech class. As a result, I started to look forward to my speeches from there on out. I gave a speech about Satchel Paige. It was 10 minutes and it was easy to me. It showed me that I can command an audience and own the room. I can make you pay attention to me without force, but through connecting to your heart with my words. In the moment, it felt like something out the Twilight Zone, an out of body experience. I was witnessing people actually paying attention to me. Life became more meaningful; I knew that I could reach people via the content I shared by way of speaking. What I didn't understand was this Africana's Studies Speech class was helping me tap into my life's calling. People were intrigued by what was about to flow from my mouth because they were going to get substance and direction from me.

It gave me confidence in a way I had never known. My 12-year-old self-lacked confidence in all facets of my life. The script flipped in that year as I exuded confidence when I had that stage and for however long the class was in session.

I would always be the only black athlete in my business management classes. I didn't have classes with the other brothas on my team. The positive thing about constantly having classes with people you don't know is that it forces you out of your comfort zone. The skills learned in my speech class served as the vehicle of transportation that allowed me to showcase my value in the room. I remember having to speak during a group project for a Human Resources class. All the other members where nervous about my part of the project in all of our meetings prior to presentation. I spoke last during the presentation and everyone in the group was stunned. Even my teacher was amazed. Here I was breaking stereotypes with the utilization of my voice.

I also had an entrepreneurial class with one of the members of the previously mentioned group. When the topic of who should speak came up she was like, "Tyler should do it, he is unreal". The other group members weren't having it and truth be told, I didn't want the spotlight. I had peace during the closure of that year. I found something outside of ball that made me whole and for that I am forever indebted to SDSU.

CHAPTER 5 "Defense"

In the sports community there is a famous saying that states "the best **defense** is a good offense". I found this quote to have an adverse effect as it relates to my life issues.

Playing the running back position, you're coached to run behind your blockers and escape the tackles of the **defense**. Offensively, I was trained to run the play given and hit each open hole hard on the football field. Seems like I had subconsciously lived my life like that.

I've come to the realization that I spent the earlier part of my life in a **defensive** stance. I'd become accustomed to not letting anyone else in, not even my own beloved family and friends. All the while, I could've opened up and asked for help, instead of internalizing and building barricades all around myself. There wasn't a real or relevant reason that I felt I had to protect myself. There was no history of abuse or traumatizing experiences that had shaped my life at that point, I just felt if I held it all in, no one would have to decipher my scattered thoughts or inner pain. The truth is, in my young and undeveloped mind, I pondered the fact that I was saving everyone else the trouble of something I wasn't at the place to verbalize. I was crying out with my mouth closed. If you are reading this page and have went through something similar you know exactly where I was.

My time in seventh grade was very different for me. 'Offense' placed an emphasis of getting to the goal line and '**defense**' was keeping people out. I think that I ended up getting pretty good with masking my feelings, like a face mask on my helmet. I felt it was beginning to become my Achilles heel as a person. My growth was really stunted during those years. Especially the latter years of college, going through everything, trying to maneuver and grow out of those teenage years followed by the transition into my 20s and adulthood.

One of the things that I kicked myself for was, if you look at all those experiences, I never opened up to anybody about what I was going through. I didn't know how and honestly, I didn't want to.

Can you believe it, I never talked to a single soul? You carry around all the excess weight, all the additional stress. I was not playing the position I 'wanted' to play. Up until my senior season, my entire time in California I played fullback instead of running back. I battled back and forth internally unhappy and broken on the inside but you try your best to win. Exterior wise, I'm a captain, a leader, excelling in school and have to have your game face on at all times. Stood in front of the team every day with a big smile on my face yet crying on the inside. Without a doubt I needed somebody to be there for me, but I could only trust myself.

TC was that guy that coaches put the underclassman with to steer them in the right direction. You got all of this being put on you while you're guarded, "Okay, this is who I'm supposed to be," but I never knew how to express everything to someone else. I was always on the **defense** with sensitive subjects in my life. When topics would hit close to the issues I was facing, I would retreat. I failed at being taught or never learned if you're broken or if you're hurting, how to express, and it all went back down to the 12-year-old boy trapped on the inside. The healing from that little boy never happened because I shielded him. See, TC guarded and covered little Tyler. I was 21 on the outside, big, strong, a leader amongst men, but internally I was emotionally behind.

Whenever I tried to tap into my inward person, it was like having a collision with a big wall of **defense** that I couldn't seem to get over. It was extremely hard to gather the keys to unlock myself from my own inner prison. Without possessing the self-care tools to conduct the inner work I needed, I remained stuck.

The beautiful thing about football is you could go out and emit a lot of stress. If somebody asked me what's going on, I can be on the **defense** with that, but I could find a source to emit and release what was plaguing me at that time without having to voice it out. Too many times to count, I let the padded practices do the talking for me. I found my temporary cure, which was football. All the while, you step off of that football field and you decompress and the little boy inside was left to himself to manage.

Actually, while attending San Diego State, those latter years were very unhappy for me. That was the time when living with multiple sclerosis became very real for me. Having this disease, I truly didn't know what was going on. I'm calm, cool, and collected, but thankfully, nobody ever said the wrong thing or did the wrong thing, because I felt like if they did, I would have blown up. As much as I was laid back, mild tempered and collected, there was a part of me that was very angry. Football was the tool that allowed me to mask it. Imagine the silent ticking of a clock to a time bomb, that was me at the time.

I had to believe that was due in a part of a lot of things that were left unaddressed which left me dealing in that moment with another crisis that I had to keep internally. More weight was added to the tons of things already mounting. Life from that point on- was a real inner war zone and a daily battle.

It was a **defensive** struggle. Standing toe-to-toe with myself, as well as the opposition of a disease, and trying to figure out how to get through the next 24 hours, felt so tired. Summer was a vigorous time. I put myself through 2- a- day practices, worked a summer job and enrolled in summer school. Ted, got me a job at Dixieline Lumber and Home Centers in National City, CA. My senior year, I even had the chance to work on the PGA Tour at Torrey Pines Golf Course. I was loading dishes during the miraculous comeback that Tiger Woods had on Rocco Mediate. I will never forget the roar of the crowd while I was carrying a crate of dirty dishes near the 18th hole. You could feel the cheers from the crowd in your chest. I'd work out at 6:00 in the morning, and then I'd come back and work out again with my teammates in the afternoon. We'd have a morning lifting and running group, an afternoon running group, and our strength coach, John, let me run in the afternoon again as long as I promised to give maximum effort. I was doing this all while living with MS. My **defense** was to work all of the time in hopes to cope with my inner issues.

Everyone thought that I was working hard or 'Tyler Campbell' was just trying to survive while feeling helpless. I always felt I was two steps behind because MS was beating me up like a heavy weight boxer striking a punching bag. I was so sad inside. I thought that I could overcome it by working out harder, which actually was more detrimental to my own health, but I didn't know that at the time. You don't know those things if you don't express or talk about them. I didn't tell my doctor any of that stuff, because I was fearful she was going to take football away. My junior/senior year, was a very tense time in my life. I was still the same person, but from a different view, I was very tense, broken and also very agitated.

Sometimes things were funny because my power clean numbers were more than my bench press numbers with MS. Power Clean would be 385 lbs, but I could only bench press 365 pounds.

I'm so thankful to the Lord that nothing ever happened, that I didn't hurt anyone during those times. I mean that wholeheartedly because I was not a small dude. I know there was so much anger that was in me, that without football, it would have been impossible to control. I just so happened to play a sport where I could release a little bit of it and blow off steam. I later discovered that I couldn't live my life in protection mode. There wasn't a shield big enough to block me from my true self. My vindication and security would only come from freeing myself from the straitjacket of defense that I placed myself in.

CHAPTER 6 "Change Of Possession "

SOMETHING FEELS OFF

The game of football is starting to get very hard for me because my body is not the same. It was if I was moving in slow motion while struggling to do the average. I'm noticing during the football season that I'm not able to keep up. It was like I wanted to do things on the field at my usual speed but I found myself doing them in twice the time. It was all because of MS. I was very lethargic. When I wasn't able to inject myself at home, I would wait until all my teammates left the locker room. Then I would go to an empty toilet stall and inject myself with my MS medication. Keeping everything hidden was a top priority for me. My roommate Matt even kept it a secret. I was a captain going into my senior year, yet being held captive by a needle.

A month after my 21st birthday, we played the last game of my junior season against BYU. I knew I was going home for either Thanksgiving or Christmas and that there wouldn't be any Bowl games during the holidays. Special teams are what really gave me an identity on the team that year. We were playing them at home. I had a great special teams game. As matter of fact, I made the first tackle of the game running down on kickoff. The returner was running down the sideline getting ready to score a touchdown. He cut it back to the middle of the field. I broke off my block and caught him. For me, it was just a culmination of the way the season was going.

THE BALL CAME OUT

The game ended with no injuries, no concussions, only normal bumps and bruises, nothing that an ice pack couldn't handle. Standard protocol was that you would go home, chill, kick it, me and my roommate, Matt. Everything was good the night before. I'd wake up the next morning like I always do. If you have any bumps and bruises as an athlete, you get to go to the training room the next day and get checked by a doctor or let the trainers see you. Normally I'd get ice and head home, but this day was going to require a different protocol than anyone else on the team.

At the time, Matt and I lived in a second-story apartment, 4896 Talmadge Park Row, right at the bottom of Montezuma, nearby the campus. Just like every other day, I woke up early, getting ready to conduct my daily routine. My whole college life had been about me waking up at 5:00 or 5:30 in the morning. Matt and I'd always been in the first weightlifting group at 6:00 a.m. I wanted to be in the earliest group because it always held me accountable for my decisions the night before. I planned with purpose. Still to this day, I wake up at 5:00 a.m., even if it's just for me to lie back down in the bed. I woke up in college without an alarm clock. I didn't need one. After PCC my body was trained that way, just like our troops that fight to defend the United States of America.

December 2, 2007, however, presented a wake-up call that I will never forget as long as I live. I remember getting up out of bed, feeling fine, maneuvering both of my feet to the floor. But as soon as I tried to stand up, I fell flat on my face. I tried to regain balance but felt like the Leaning Tower of Pisa, your boy leaned, and fell face down to the floor at side of the bed. My first initial thought was, "What in the world is going on?" My thought process was, "Okay, try to get up again." I couldn't. I tried to get up again and fell over. I noticed that the right side of my body was totally numb. No pain, just a tingling sensation, and I couldn't feel anything. I couldn't even feel the warmth of the carpet underneath my right foot. I did my best to feel something but no matter how hard I tried I felt nothing except pins and needles pulsating down to my toes. Then when I tried to get up on the left side, I fell over again. This time, I couldn't even talk. My voice went mute. It was like my tongue became very fat in my mouth and was gaging me. The words wouldn't come out despite the fact that I felt my lips moving.

I noticed that my whole equilibrium was totally shot. Nothing mechanically, nothing motorized, nothing verbally was working properly. I laid there for a while, because I was just trying to figure out what was going on. It was still dark outside, early in the morning and here I was unable to use any of my motor functions. Completely unaware and caught off guard, I looked to the ceiling and began staring into space.

I gave it some time, hoping that things would get better. I thought about trying to position myself up against the wall but I elected to just lay there. In that moment, I faced a hard reality. I came face to face with a potential outcome. What if I can't play football anymore? I remember the butterflies in my stomach and the sweat running down my face as if it was all a dream.

A few moments later, I noticed that my roommate, Matt, was getting up. I don't know what time it was but it was later that morning. I finally was able to muster up enough strength to raise my voice and yell for Matt. I let him know that something was 'off' with my body. It took some time but I was able to get myself dressed. After that, we got to the training room and I let the trainers know that something was wrong. Obviously, they could see that my motor functioning was way off. My speech was still slurred and forming sentences was a real chore. The right side of my body still wasn't working. They asked me if I was concussed or not. My answer was obviously, NO.

Up until that point, I had never seen the team doctor in all of my college career, except for coming into that year as a high blood pressure patient. I got put on high blood pressure medication because hypertension is prevalent in my family. It was hereditary. That was my first time failing physically, really. I did not pass the blood pressure check and had been placed on blood pressure medication.

The team doctor gave me the motor skills test, touch your finger to your nose and follow his hand. The doctor was positioning his hand somewhere, you'd touch your nose, and then try to touch his hand, while doing it in a straight line. Every single time I went to touch it, I saw where his hand was but I'm not touching it. I'm telling my right hand where to go, but it wouldn't connect. Next I was instructed to walk in a straight line. It looked like I was drunk, because I couldn't do it. Staggering, I fell over. By this time, I had a little bit more strength. In my head, I can see the doctor, I'm walking towards him, but my body is doing something totally different. He said, "I'll be right back."

He went into his office for some time, and I was sitting outside the office in a chair. Within that time, Matt came in worried. I couldn't answer his questions of, "What happened to you?" I didn't know the answer myself. My head felt dizzy. The doctor came back out and gave me a piece of paper and he said, "There is a neurologist that you need to call so you can book an appointment, at Scripps La Jolla Memorial Hospital, in La Jolla, California. They'll help you try to figure out what this is." Now, I've become even more terrified because I got passed off from trainer, to team doctor and now neurologist. Normally, the team doctor was the end road to getting an answer as an athlete. Instead, I was preparing to head to a hospital in a very prestigious part of California that was away from my normal surroundings.

La Jolla, is a very beautiful city that tourists often visit. You go there to see the seals and enjoy the beach community. I used to come to La Jolla so I could visit a place called Mount Solidad. It is a big mountain that once had a huge cross on the top. I used to go over there and look over all of La Jolla. It served as a place where my dreams could be set free without judgement.

I would get on top that mountain and look out and see the ocean and think about all the stuff that I have been through that got me to this point in life. I left Austin, Texas in 2004 and now here I was in San Diego, California. This was the place that I always wanted to go to but didn't know which path to take to get there. It was in these moments of reflection, that I would hear God for myself saying, "I didn't bring you this far to leave you. Trust and believe, Tyler, I have always been there and will continue to be there for you, son." The mountain always recharged me and gave me a fresh perspective. I went up to the top of the mountain like Clark Kent but came down like Superman ready to represent.

Under normal circumstances I came to this city, at my leisure, just to get a piece of a peace of mind without going through hell. But now, it was different. I was going to La Jolla to go to a hospital. Now I'm starting to get a little bit scared. I didn't tell my family because I didn't want to tell them until I knew exactly what was going on with me.

I drove myself to La Jolla with the car my father had given me a year prior. Can you imagine driving to your own emergency medical appointment? The funny thing is I drove all the way there using my left foot, because my right wouldn't work. That probably wasn't safe, but I drove with my left foot because I had developed drop foot. I couldn't make my foot dorsal. I hobbled my way up there dragging my right foot. As soon as I walked in the building, I searched the directory and found my neurologist's office. I didn't understand the impact. As soon as I walked in, I noticed there were diagrams of the human brain all over the place.

I remember signing my name at the check in window then I sat down. An elderly white woman was there and she said, "Son, what are you doing here?" I said, "Honestly ma'am, I don't know. They say there might be something wrong up here (I pointed to my head) that we can figure out today." She was staring at me, "You're too young to be here." As soon as she said, those words, the nurse called out, "Tyler Campbell." It was just the progression of knowing that you're not about to get good news. I don't know everything, but this isn't going to be like my normal in-and-out doctor's appointment. Mentally, by this time in my life I had been through so many ups and downs, whatever news the neurologist was to give me, I'm going to figure this new life out. That's your typical athlete mindset. Whatever it is, we get some pills and some direction then we take care of the rest. At this time, I am also thinking they will probably give me some physical exercise to do as well. I was even thinking of everything I could to stay positive, but a small part of me said, 'Will it be ok?'

I went back there to see the doctor and she was a short lady. I positioned myself as I sat on the patients' table. The nurse had already taken all my vitals. When the doctor opened the door, she was walking backwards like she's talking to somebody, and she's backing up to me. She couldn't see me. I tried to look calm, keeping my composure. When she turned around and saw me, her eyes jumped.

I read people very well. I pay very close attention to their body movements and nonverbal communication. I'm very cerebral like that. I read your body language. Pop used to say, "You can figure out a person," all the time growing up, "by the way, they carry themselves, and their body language will tell you everything you need to know about a person." I always found truth with that and it became very handy.

When she spotted me on the table, her eyes jumped. It was like, "I'm not expecting to see this type of patient." I was close to 230 pounds and young. She gave me the same test that the team doctor put me through, and I failed every single one of them, just like I did at the school. Nothing had changed in two days.

She asked me if I lived near the area. And I replied, "No, ma'am, I'm a college student. I play football at San Diego State University. I'm here all by myself." She was surprised, "You don't have any family?" I looked down, "No ma'am, not here. Everybody's back in Texas." I looked into her eyes. She sighed and continued, "I'm going to give you a spinal tap, because I think I know what this might be." They took out a long needle and they put it into my spinal cord, from there they extracted my spinal fluid. It did not take long for testing. It came back a little later that day. She made me call my mom after the test. My mom is actually a former registered nurse. She had medical background before she started getting into her own individual work. My mom spoke to her and then my mother asked me to listen to everything the doctor was telling me to do. Then she said, she wanted to talk about the rest when I got back home. Next the doctor said, clearly worried and her eyes read through me, "I think this might be multiple sclerosis. We'll clarify that through the spinal tap. I'm also going recommend that you go get some MRIs done at the imaging center near your school. It was either the same day or the next day to get the MRI. I can't really remember. She continued, "We'll call you with the results of everything, and we'll let you know the next steps." I then headed back to my apartment. My mom was like, "This multiple sclerosis thing, if this is potentially it, Tyler, this is really serious. You can't play with any of this, and you have to do exactly what she says." It's still up in the air. I then proceed to get my imaging done. Then that next day, the nurse calls me. She says, "You got to come back up here." So I drive back to La Jolla and the doctor says, "This is multiple sclerosis." She does her best to explain everything. It was a blur but my only response was, "Can I still play football with it?" That was my only question. I said, "Okay, I got this brain thing. I got holes on my brain". She says it's an autoimmune disease. I don't know what that is. There's fatigue that can come with this disease. There's paralysis, which I've experienced, that comes with this disease. There's constant pain, all the bad things of multiple sclerosis. I looked at her and asked, "So can I still play football?" She continued after a while, studying my face, "I've never had an athlete as a patient before. I've never seen anybody like you before." I knew that also meant color-wise, as well as physique-wise, because I did my homework after that. I found out that MS, at that time in 2007, was largely a white woman's disease. That's what it was. When I did my research, I didn't find anybody like me, except Montel Williams, the talk show host. At that moment, I was like, "Cool, because I can football with this disease. She'll support me, I can be like her guinea pig. She never had anybody like me before. As long as I show that I'm doing okay, she won't strip the ball away from me." That was my mindset. Everything for me is football, football, football, football. I asked if I could still play ball? She said, "Yes, but if you have a relapse with the disease, we're going to have to take the game away from you, because if not, there is a possibility that you could spend the rest of your life in a wheelchair." She saw that MS has attacked my body aggressively. I, on the other hand, had no clue, I was oblivious to it. Oddly enough it took over 10 years for me to learn MS is more aggressive in black men than other races and genders for some reason. This disease was thrown into my lap at the age of 21. I said, "Playing football, that's a gamble I'm willing to take." I worked so hard to get to SDSU. I had been through so much. I earned a scholarship. I was graduating early from school that spring with my business management degree. I signed a letter of intent on the dotted line and that meant I made a commitment to San Diego State University. Commitment means something. I was taught that from my father early on in life, "You make a commitment; you follow through with that commitment, no matter how dark it looks." I signed a letter of intent. That was a commitment.

Once I knew that, she told me it was going to be okay. I never thought I wasn't going to play football. I never even questioned it. She said, "You got to give yourself shots every single day in different parts of your body. We're going to give you steroids." When she said steroids, I was startled, I said, "Ma'am, I'm a Division I athlete. I can't take steroids." She stole a glance at the papers and said, "Nah, it isn't that type of party, Tyler. These are legal steroids." I was getting ready to go into my finals in December. "You said I can play football, then what do we do about this, because my hand is not responding? Some of my finals are going to be written. She said, "We're going to send a nurse by your apartment. They're going to show you how to administer your own steroids. After the steroids, you'll get your own infusion medication that you will administer for yourself, directly, for your MS. For now, we'll give you steroids to try to jumpstart your body." The steroids worked like magic, except for making my right arm work. I took my finals left-handed. My last final was in essay form. I tried my best, but had to do it left-handed. Just gripping the pencil was a tall task. I was the last one to finish the essay. I remember people would look at me funny when I was going to class on campus. My right leg was dragging. I had developed a stutter. I had an uncontrollable twitch. That was the other side of MS. My twitch was similar to that of Abdul Rauf who used to play for the Denver Nuggets back in the day. I guess it was just a side effect, but I never talked to my coaches about any of this MS stuff. I told the trainers, and I took my injections on time. I did do one shot in front of them, them being the trainers. I wanted to let them know or make sure that I was injecting myself the right way and nothing was getting infected. The injections were not fun, but I got used to it. The sites would rotate every day. I would have to inject my arms, quads, hips, butt cheeks, as well as my abdominal area. It was like a whirlwind. I didn't really understand what exactly was happening. I just knew it was this other thing, and you play football with this thing. I didn't tell my teachers; I didn't want to make excuses or draw attention. I wasn't to that point where I could share with you my whole life story about what I had. I wasn't that type of person. I wanted to always be a regular guy who played ball, went to school, and kicked it. This was the starting point of my hard reality.

Days passed and I still didn't tell my coaches about my illness. The beautiful thing about it was, I passed all my finals that semester with A and B grades. I will never forget the IV process (Intravenous therapy). I would take out my steroid balls and plug them into my IV that was administered by the nurse who came by the house. She showed me how to administer my own IV steroids, crazy right.

Little by little I started doing more research on MS to broaden my knowledge. What I found was that there were no Black people that I knew of or could find or could call or could research, outside of Montel Williams, especially Black males to be specific; my soul was yearning for something that was nonexistent, and I felt more isolated. My dad would be the one to tell me it was going to be okay. I know it crushed him, because he didn't understand what this MS stuff was either and he couldn't help me. I had to figure this out on my own. Pop was on the outside looking in with this one. I yearned for a Black male who could tell me, "You got this." A black male that could offer insight to make me feel like, "Yeah, he did it, I can too." Montel Williams was a star and all the way on the other side of the country, so I wasn't going to have a conversation with him about MS. What my soul yearned for the most, I couldn't provide. I did, however, make a promise to myself that, during the early part of my life, I won't let another person of color not be able to find out about me with this MS thing. I knew what it was like to hope to find that person. Then I realized I had to be that person so another black male could say "Okay, Tyler did it and is doing it big, so can I." That was my mindset with MS at that time. One of my most prize possessions was my body. I took pride in my dedication to train and keep my physical physic in game ready condition. In turn, when MS hit me it felt like it had possessed my body and for a moment I lost complete control.

CHAPTER 7 "UNDRAFTED"

It was like life had circled back to repeat itself after my Senior year of college ended. Once again, I watched my peers near and from afar be highly recruited by pro football scouts and analysts. I looked on from the sideline but unlike times in the past, I was determined to play football at the pro level.

I spoke with my mom and dad about my dream to play in the NFL. No matter what, I wanted their blessing and support. They both agreed to let me pursue my dream with the promise to get a job if it didn't work out.

Without question or apprehension, I was ready to go to the next level. During my senior season, I had no relapses or anything that set me back from playing football. I made it through the season just fine. I felt that, if I can just workout, everything will be okay. The football off-season training regimen is different than an actual season. The biggest difference is that you don't have to deal with anyone hitting your body. Many of my teammates had their own sports agents because they had a much better college resume than me. My Pop said, "Do you know how to read and do you know how to write? Listen, the only way you are going to make it into the National Football League is, if you're a free agent anyway. You're not about to get drafted by anyone. You don't have enough film. You have got to play politics. The league is all about politics, point blank. So you got a last name. Use that and get your body in the best of shape possible."

What he said next was what kept me lifted throughout my training, "Tyler you've played many positions in college. That makes you versatile and a rare commodity. The only way you're going to make the team is if you play special teams." He kept it real. He was like, "Can you block now?". "Yeah, I spent the last five years of my life in California doing nothing but blocking." He went on with my answer, "Ok son, so drop the weight and try to go in as a running back. Then if they tell you to pick up weight, you can do that, and you can play fullback. No matter what, you will have to play special teams. Drop the weight. Get the 40 yard dash time where it needs to be. You're already naturally strong. We are wired that way."

We are wired that way, I started repeating that phrase while I simultaneously looked back over my life. I had my first dunk when I was in ninth grade. I was 14 years old. We are wired that way athletically. I'll never forget the closing piece of our conversation that day. He said, "What you are preparing for is a swimsuit contest. People aren't doing anything but looking at the size of your legs, width of your shoulders, size of your butt, length of your hands and overall body type. It is beauty pageant and you have to show up and entertain".

Coach David "Ottie" Ohton was another strength and conditioning coach at SDSU with a rich history tied to his name. I sought after him when training for the next level and best of all, it was free. He didn't train us in football, but he was notorious for helping guys like Marshall Faulk, Robert Griffin, Will Demps, JR Tolver, Kabeer and Akbar Gbaja-Biamila and Kirk Morrison. Those are just a few of the names. I mean, the man's resume was larger than life. I felt as if I was walking in the legacy of so many great Aztecs who came before me. We may not have always had great football teams, but we sure would put lots of guys in the NFL over the years. The older cats that came before me worked out with Coach

O. He heard through the grapevine that I was a hard worker. He said, "I'll train you, because I know you will show up. But if you're late one time, you are out. That a deal?" My response was easy and without hesitation. "Yes Sir!"

He had two other cats (Jerome and Scottie) who were former SDSU alumni that always worked out with him in the early a.m. hours. As a matter of fact, Jerome was still playing ball in the CFL during this time. Training with Coach O reminded me of a powerful lesson in life that I knew of but needed a fresh reminder. It was that people are watching you, even when you don't think anyone's paying attention. So the question you then must ask yourself is, what product are you putting out for people to see? Scottie and Jerome said, "we have seen you work, come in and get with Coach O. Don't do anything else but what he says and we will push you." My teammates Josh and J-Shaw joined me as well. Shaw, unfortunately didn't last long. He got kicked out. Actually, I went to go pick him up during one of our first workouts because he didn't have a ride. I was on that 'no man left behind' stuff so I told him I would come scoop him up. I almost got thrown out of Coach O's workouts because I went to go pick him up and we were late. Lesson learned that day, as bad as it sounded, yo I had to be selfish at this time in my life and look out for me.

It was the hardest I've ever worked out in my life. I was burning so many calories, I felt like I was always starving. As a result, I had to bring protein shakes into my daily routine. Plus, I wanted to put on good weight with lean muscle. I needed to be chiseled, but not look like a body builder. The unfortunate part about this entire process was that I had to eat my own cooking. What I am trying to say is that all my food was disgusting. My 3 meats on rotation were turkey, chicken and fish. I would do my shopping at 'Food 4 Less' off University Ave and on the weekends head to Costco in Mission Valley with Matt for my chicken. I had a tight budget so I ate the same few meals every day for 3 months. I dropped the weight and got down to 212 lbs. to get faster.

TYLER CAMPBELL

I started running 4.5's in the 40-yard dash consistently. I was so excited because this was the fastest I had ever been in my life. No cap.

Coach McDaniel called me into his office while I was training at the school. He said, "Tyler, for this Pro Day, what do you think if I allow somebody who's a native of San Diego to come in, it'll pull more scouts? It'll help be more beneficial for you as a running back."

The person he was referring to was future Houston Texans running back Arian Foster. He played his college ball at Tennessee, but came home to do his Pro Day in San Diego. He had already done the NFL Combine and was coming back to test better in a few drills. I told Coach Mac to bring him in, competition was something I never shied away from. It was only going to help and trust me I needed all the help I could get. The best part was that my dad and brother came to support me. Again, I also understood the politics of the day. I may not have had a sports agent, but I had to play whatever card I could to gather interest. It was go hard or go home. The scouts knew who Earl Campbell was. It was a legendary feat for Pop to be sitting out there on the field in his wheelchair for my Pro Day. The NFL community knew my dad was in bad physical shape. He didn't travel much back then because it caused so much pain. I also understood that, having him there was special. Point being, when I needed my father, he showed up every single time. He wasn't just present, but more importantly he made his presence felt. There is a big difference between the two.

The morning of my pro day, I felt like I was going to kill it. I'm nervous, but I feel like I'm going to kill it. I think I woke up at four something in the morning. Coach O gave Josh and I a schedule by-the-minute of what we were supposed to be doing leading up to the start of the event. The wake up, the stretches, even what to eat and the quantities of it. No lie, I even had a two-pound weight tucked in my tights. Every pound counts and 'by any means necessary' was my motto! I squeezed my shoulder blades tight when they were doing my reach, that way my vertical leap would be higher.

Every inch matters for this 'beauty pageant'. My test numbers were 'ok' but I had done better before. On the bench press, I topped out at 24 reps of 225 lbs. I had a 38-inch vertical and 10-foot broad jump. On my first 40-yard dash, I reaggravated my injured right hip flexor. An injury that occurred earlier that week, but I still managed to run a 4.63. No excuses; everybody plays this game hurt.

I remember a scout from the New York Jets. A tall Black gentleman. He was the running backs' coach for them. He tapped me on my shoulder before outside drills started. He asked, "Are you related to Earl Campbell?" I said, "Yes, sir, that's my father." He said, "I got a crazy story for you. I'm here to see Arian Foster, but I have to tell you this. I went to University of Texas. I met your father when I came there on a recruiting trip, and he is the reason why I went to UT. I don't think all these people know that your dad is Earl Campbell." I saw many others who kept looking at my father. It was good to see all the love and respect that was coming his way. As for me, I knew my journey toward a goal was always going to be hard with a road less traveled. Even if somebody told me I would have to go to Canada or overseas, I was cool with that, because that was my life. I was used to getting it out the mud. All I wanted was an opportunity. Overall, I had a great showing. I gave it everything that I had out there on the field. I just knew that my phone was going to get ready to ring, not on Draft Day, but after Draft Day.

The Pro Day was big, but the real highlight was my father coming out as well for my first charity function that evening. My teammate Josh and I put a fundraiser together called Fairways Fore Kids. We wanted to help a local school get greater resources. I always volunteered at this school while I was at State and it was called Encanto Elementary. Josh and I had no idea how to put together an event. All we had was our hustle and a dream. We were connected to Mary B, an

Executive Producer at Pro Player Foundation. I knew she had to be dope because no one knew her last name. Mary took Josh and I under her wing and believed in our dream. She was kind enough to introduce us into her circle and that meant the world. She was like a second mom to Josh and I. So not only were we working out in the off season, but we were also making the transition to philanthropy. We were raising money, meeting people in San Diego and putting together our first ever charity golf tournament called 'Fairways Fore Kids'.

So many within the city showed up to our gathering Saturday and tournament on Sunday. People like NFL Hall of Famer Charlie Joiner and Az Zahir Hakim a former Aztec and Super Bowl Champion with the St. Louis Rams. Man, what a weekend, what a blessing. I received the opportunity to work out for the NFL in my father's presence. The following two days were full of love and support for an Elementary school in need. The icing on the cake was that some of the kids from Encanto got to come to the golf course and be exposed to something new. They looked everywhere in awe, which melted every heart. They saw athletes who were there for them. They were shown this other part of SD, which I'm sure, many of them had never seen, but people unified themselves right here for them. The school didn't believe Josh and I could pull this off. Who could blame them, we were just two student athletes who wanted to help kids and leave something in the soil for the students at Encanto Elementary.

CHAPTER 8 "SPECIAL TEAMS"

You never have to motivate me to put in the work for something, you just don't. I think that's my secret sauce that I take the most pride in. You may be more talented, but you will have to drag me by my limbs from the task at hand and put me on my death bed before I let you outwork me. You may be more gifted but you are going to look at me and say, why won't he just quit. I'm not going to afford you that opportunity in life. I will not.

In the beginning, I started off with saying one of my most prized attributes is my heart and that springs me up to my feet because I get really excited about the matters of the heart. My heart is the core and the true motive of who I am as a man. However, the more I've dove into myself or analyzed myself, I realized, it's never been my talent alone though blessed by the Creator. I looked at everything under a microscope, the rollercoaster that I've been on. My life has produced an unstoppable *work ethic*. For instance, I like to think of my life as a construction site. I've had to get my shovel, put on the hard hat, and just go out and get it. I've been around individuals, who were always more talented than me. I was never the most gifted or athletic in the locker room. Tyler wasn't the fastest, strongest, tallest, or the one with the highest football IQ. It was almost as if the Good Lord was always telling me from the beginning, "You're not going to have what other people have. So you've got to live your life with blinders on to the mess, to the distractions or even the politics in sports. You don't have that afforded athletic opportunity and availability to not give your all. That's not how I designed you. But what I have given you is the willingness to be consistent and have a work ethic about yourself".

If I have my eyes fixated on something, I'm all systems go. MS or not, I can go. As long as my heart is in the right place.

I can tell you that, I will die before I am a no-show or I let you down. That's the same mindset I exhibited around my teammates. That is what took me overboard in the classroom because I wasn't the smartest in the room, but what I did was, I put the hours in and I would go to study hall for hours or roll to the library by myself. When it came to friendships, I tried to do my best to add value. If you tell me something, I'm going to remember it and work towards implementing what was needed on my part to be of any help. TC was and is going to work to showcase to you that I value our relationship. My work ethic, when I look back over my life, it is the only thing that separates me from others. It started earlier in life when I got tired of being made fun of, when my mother, father and brother told me, "you've got to work for what you want". Those words 'work for what you want' took any rights to privilege out of my mentality. Now I am walking into things and it's like, no, I don't know how to do this, or no, I don't know how to do that, but I go in learn it and master it. When I learned something new, no matter the subject, for lack of a better phrase, it's 'game over' because I'm going to work while you're asleep. I can play that constant work game with myself every time and I never get tired of it. I'm 35 years old, living with MS, but I am still playing the same game as that little 12 year old boy, 13 year old adolescent, high school teenage boy and a college student athlete. It is the same game with different scenery.

When our strength coaches would tell me that I have got to stop working so hard or what was I going to do at the gym on my own for those off season 2-a-day workouts, my response would be that I wanted to be better than last year. Why did I graduate college early? Because I promised my mom that I wasn't coming home without a degree. With that vow, I worked and I overloaded myself to get it done. If hard work was a condiment it would be my secret sauce. I looked back over my life and my heart was always in the right place. You can never take away my work ethic. That was a decision that I made and a commitment that I tattooed to myself.

To be completely honest, the work principles came naturally once I activated them. As I get older and understand my history, I realized that it just goes hand-in-hand and it has nothing to do with Earl Campbell. If you talked to my dad's 10 other brothers and sisters, and if you talked to his mother and if you talked to anybody that I was raised around, they will tell you that my father was the laziest Campbell. When he went to work in the rose fields, he didn't work. He tried to hide. When they were picking cotton, he tried to find an undisclosed location away from work. The reason why he made it in the National Football League was simply so he wouldn't have to pick cotton or work on a share-croppers land anymore. That was his motivation because he didn't like waking up early. In hindsight, I'm so happy my dad didn't get comfortable laying in the cotton fields but ran onto the football fields instead. There is a show on PBS called Genealogy Roadshow and that is how I really tapped into my family roots. After I finished college my dad was on the first season of the show. What they did was tap into all the records on my dad's side of the family. As I stated earlier on in the book, my dad only knew so much about his family. His dad died on him when he was young and he came from very humble beginnings in Tyler, TX. Their original house was burned down to ashes and with that the family lost a lot of historic documents and family photos. Genealogy Roadshow did coverage on those things as well. That is how I got my answers of the first ever Campbell. They said there was a boy between eight to ten years old, from either Alabama or Georgia, because they didn't have exact slave records at the time. Somehow that little boy, when slavery was abolished, made his way to Texas, Tyler, Texas. That little boy worked land, settled down and had a family. His wife gave birth to a child that became the worker of that land. One of his children became the owner of that land and he was my Great-Great-Grandfather. This made him one of the first few black landowners in Smith county. I know it took some form of grit, some form of will, some form of determination to get yourself from Alabama or Georgia when slavery was abolished all the way to Texas, and watch this, when he got to Texas, slavery was still going on because we were two years behind the rest of the country. That's why we celebrate June 19th or Juneteenth, which is the celebration of slavery being abolished in Texas. I've never seen him nor have I heard about him. Nobody even had a picture of him. He was the ancestor who lives in memories.

My family owned land despite a suppressed environment. That took work and determination to get that land. My father's dad, BC Campbell, was one of the few members of the Black Army Air Corps to be present on D-Day. He never spoke about it to anyone when he came back from the war. PBS had the documentations of all of this in the records they pulled up. This was my family's rich history that we never knew about. So you see, I come from a family of extremely hard workers. That's why it comes natural for me. It's like the reflection from a crystal glass mirror. I come from a line of heroes because my father's dad was there on D-Day. The Campbells were heroes long before Earl Campbell stepped foot on a football field, he was just the icing on the cake. So when I look at my life now, the way that I lived made sense. I am a byproduct of the lineage that existed before I was even thought of. I now know why I am crafted this way because it's hardwired in my DNA.

When I left high school, I grew more confident. Not arrogant but confident. I didn't know everything. I don't know how it all came about, but I learned I could put the work in to catch me up to wherever I needed to go. Not because anyone gave me anything or did something in particular for me. It's because if you showed me a rocky path to success, I'm going to go to the stone and grind that thing to perfection or until it became a perfect sphere. I have a peace when I do it. I'm happy when I work hard because I know I'm doing what others feel they don't have time to do. I know I'm doing what others take for granted.

It took me years to realize what I want you to grasp in a couple of sentences throughout this book. I thought I was just a part of a football team. I didn't know God was teaching me practical lessons in seasons. Meaning, my ability to excel on Special Teams in sports while others looked down on it, this was the Lord's way of showing me I was on His team. In other words, what God was doing naturally in my life was symbolic or prophetic to who I was and foreshadowing my divine purpose. Man isn't that special! Being a fruit from an elite and amazing family tree showed me how exceptional I was, as well as clearly illustrated that my roots run deep.

When you leave this page, I want you to be thinking about the stuff that you just read. As a matter of fact, I've opened up my life and history. I pushed myself because I've got to do my due diligence to help everyone who reads this book to see how teamwork works. My friend I want you to know that you are a part of a Special Team. You're not just a happen stance or a person merely living day to day. There's something unusual, distinctive, exceptional, particular, different, extraordinary, superior, and specific about you.

CHAPTER 9 "THE OFF SEASON"

Every season comes to an end, it is an unspoken law. It doesn't stay winter, fall, summer or spring forever. That was said throughout the game of football regardless of if you had a winning or losing season, it always came to an end.

Resulting from the toll that MS was having on my body I returned to the familiar. I moved back to Texas and during that time I had to learn how to walk and talk again. It was if I had to relive my toddler years as a full grown adult.

Wheelchair bound, I struggled to do what used to come to me naturally. I'd never been in a wheelchair before, I was a born and raised athlete. When MS happened that last time, I found myself in the hospital; they were getting ready to take football away from me forever. I looked at the doctor and said, "when one door closes, another one opens and I'm going to be okay". Still to this day, I can't tell you where those words came from. The giant on the inside of me spoke from a deep place. Mary B can attest to this because she was in a chair in my hospital room.

When my mother arrived after my departure from the hospital, days were presented where she had to help feed me. I remember racking with pain and crying out to my mother screaming, "why me" while she was at the foot of my bed. I did everything right. I'd not made any more mistakes. I didn't have drinking problems. Then my mom read the story of Paul and his thorn in the Bible, and how he pleaded with God to take it away. Despite Paul's pleading God never removed the thorn. My mother, being the rock that she is, looked at me square in my face and said, "I don't know what MS is to you. But I feel like it's what Paul's thorn in his flesh was for him. God may not remove it from you because he needs to use it in you." Those words pierced the doubt and illuminated hope on the inside of me.

I'd be remised if I didn't pause sharing my story to tell somebody on the other side of this book who has been praying for God to move the obstruction. It won't be liked but it will be needed. The thorn (temporary, hurt, only revealing newness) is the prelude that better is here. My friend, if you can see past the pain, you'll realize that if God allowed it to be stuck in or on you, leave it there, He has a plan.

I was having issues with erectile dysfunction, just another thing that your 22-year-old self shouldn't have to face. I was really lost in this maze of MS. I didn't know what the next steps in life were. I didn't know if I was going to make it out of a wheelchair. This was my new life.

He could have hired a driver but my dad would physically drive me to physical therapy in Cedar Park, Texas at Tillman Physical Therapy Center. Dad just didn't spectate he participated in physical therapy with me. I'm emotional and fighting back tears as I reminisce because my dad had four back surgeries and knee surgeries. He's been through so much in his life due to the toll football had on his body. He cried nightly but my dad would get himself up, get down the stairs in a two-story home and he would take me, the kid with all these issues stimming from MS to physical therapy. I was working and my dad was working alongside me. I used to say to myself, "TC, you said you had a work ethic. Now look at your dad. He is 54 years old and he's crying at night because he is in so much pain. But he is here doing physical therapy with you at Tillman Physical Therapy."

I went home in 2009 and the rehab process took about a year. I was in therapy, learning how to write, learning how to talk, learning how to walk and finding my own independence. Then after all those tears the Good Lord shed his grace on me through Shana Watson in the summer of 2010. Shana moved to Texas. I was down on one knee in no time asking her to marry me because she was one of my best friends from college. Think back a couple chapters when I mentioned we didn't see eye to eye. Over time at SDSU I developed a greater understanding of her. I started calling her 'Ms. Watson' in college. We were always butting heads. I said to myself, "You need to show her a level of respect as a woman that she's probably never seen before." I'm from the South. So we say, 'ma'am or miss'. I let her know that as a man I am showing you kindness and respect not because I want something from you. I'm doing these things because I genuinely respect you as a woman. Like, *I see you.* I see your heart. Everyone else saw Shana, but I saw Ms. Watson.

When I made changes to my approach towards her, we became the best of friends. She was one of the few people who came up there to see me in the hospital. You'll find out the depth of friendship when you have no legs to stand on; a dependable friend steps in right on time. That was Ms. Watson. So when Shana came down to Texas for the final track meet of her college career. I helped her move in. Sidebar, she was a total beast in the long and triple jump when at State. By this time, I could drive, I happily informed her of that.

When I saw her in the hotel at the Hilton in downtown Austin, a day or two prior to us leaving for Dallas, I knew that something was different. I had never seen her bright aurora like this. I felt something unique in my spirit. I remember driving to Dallas and dropping her off but I didn't want her to leave. After the drop off, I drove to East Texas to be amongst family and gain peace; it was a drive that I made frequently upon regaining the freedom to get behind the wheel. I started riding horses with my cousin Victor in Tyler on weekends. Horses were therapy for me, hippotherapy is what they call it. My dad introduced me to it. It helped my blood circulation and really got the neurons in my brain firing on all cylinders. Horses made me happy and brought me a much needed escape any of life's troubles.

Ms. Watson would drive down from Dallas to Tyler and spend time with my family in East Texas. We would do trail rides together. As a matter of fact, horses brought us closer to one another. Things were happening so fast. A love that we had never known started to reveal itself. We decided to spend time away from each other as a result. The love was becoming so powerful we wanted to spend time in prayer to see if it was what God wanted us to pursue. It was in those moments I knew I did not want to be without her by my side. I loved her and I wanted to spend the rest of my life with her. It wasn't up to me though. The ball wasn't in my hands. It was up to Ms. Watson and God now. We met at my Grandmother's house in Tyler like we had been doing prior to the break. She took me into my Aunt Margret's room and the lights were out. She instructed me to sit in the chair and take my shoes off. I didn't know what was going on. Then she started washing my feet. If you know the Bible, this gesture was the ultimate sign of humility and respect. She was saying that she entrusted me with her heart and would be allowing me to lead us down this path toward marriage. If you know my wife and what she has been through, only then can you understand why this was such a privilege and special moment for me. How this event took so much faith for her to carry out. The gesture also meant we had a mutual understanding that we were working toward marriage. Our friendship meant too much to risk it for anything less.

November 7, 2010 was the date I decided it was time to ask Ms. Watson to marry me. Interestingly enough I was going through a MS relapse at the same time. I could barely get down on one knee without falling over. My heart was beating through my chest. What if she says 'no'? What if my disease is scaring her? Thankfully, she responded with a resounding 'yes'. God said, "Did you forget that this is the woman who has already seen you at your worst? You have nothing to be ashamed of so count it all joy." We got married just under a year later on September 16, 2011. Asking this amazing woman of God to marry me will always be the easiest and best decision I have ever made. I often remind her of that still to this day. No hesitation and no regrets, when you know, you know.

I felt life shifting in a new direction. Mary B, hit me up and said, "Tyler, I've got a phone call from the National MS Society. They want you to tell your story. Do you mind telling your story?" I asked if it was going to help anyone. She said, "Absolutely. Best of all, it'll be at their national conference and watch this: It will be in Dallas, Texas. You don't even have to drive far."

God had strategically put things in order for me to get ready for the blessing that he was opening up to me, if that makes sense. When I got on stage for rehearsal, I was immediately asked, "Do you need a teleprompter?"

I denied, "Absolutely not. No ma'am." She asked, "Have you ever publicly spoken before?" I said, "I did it in college during a speech class." She said, "Well, there's going to be 700 some odd people here." I politely said, "Ma'am, but what I have to give you is from my heart, I can't do a teleprompter. It's not going to sound good. I'll sound like Mush-Mouth from Fat Albert". The night of the event took place in a hotel at DFW Airport. It was filled with people. The ballroom was packed. She wasn't lying.

It was crazy because I knew in that moment this is what I always longed for, but could never find. I knew that somewhere in that audience they were recording my speech for the MS Society. It was going to give access to a black male somewhere around this country, diagnosed with MS, a story to cling to.

I was going to be that face for them because I knew what it was like to not find that face. That was one of the greatest feelings. Still to this day, it was a better feeling than scoring a touchdown. It was God's making and an understanding for me, where I saw that, quite frankly, this is what you're really supposed to be doing, my son. Football was just the talent to help you get the room. Public Speaking was the gift that will make you stay there.

That's when it all started to change. In the beginning, I did not know that you could get paid for speaking engagements. I did not know that people paid you for this because I come from a place of service. So when I do what I do, it genuinely is from a place of love and sincerity from my heart. I noticed that I fell in love with this more than studying a playbook. It was like discovering a new part of myself, and that interested me.

Thanks to Mary B, helping to guide me into the business of public speaking, I, eventually started speaking in the pharmaceutical realm because of my MS. Some speakers work all of their lives to get there. I got there in my mid-20s. No professional background or curriculum. Just a heart to serve. That's why it would catch me completely off guard when people would come up to me saying, "We've been through a lot of speakers, we've had a lot of functions, yours will always stick out." I would say to myself internally, "This has to be a dream, they can't be talking about me."

That's why I tell people, just work with what you have, because what you have is enough. Run your own race and stop worrying about what somebody else is doing, because you can't make the world better if you're not being who you are called to be. When you answer the call, then that's your submission to the Lord. This further reveals your obedience to Him and after that He will take care of the rest. I am nothing special. I was just being obedient and willing. Today, I have a radio show on 104.9 The Horn FM in Austin. I have no radio background but my show is the number one show on

TYLER CAMPBELL

Saturdays at the station. It doesn't make sense. I wish I could say it does but the only thing that I do know is that with this gift, it is my duty to nurture it.

I registered for Eric Thomas' Game Changers Speaking Program, ET, the number 1 motivational speaker in the world. The world loves him as a speaker. I love him as a husband and as a father. I don't think people talk about that enough. I enrolled in the program because in order to become good at something, you've got to get around people who are already the best at that very thing. The program had an in-person speakers boot camp at ET's church called APOC in Grand Ledge, MI. All speakers had to give a 6-minute speech and by the grace of God, I was the only speaker over those two days to get a standing ovation from the crowd. Even our coaches, Kantis, Coach Val and CJ were impressed. We all have been given a light but it's up to us to let it shine.

The speech I made there that day will always hold a special place in my heart.

When CJ threw up his arms and said, "I don't really even have much to critique you on. You're one of my favorite type of speakers. That type of speaker, when you speak, you just kind of go with whatever it is that they are talking about because you like it." For me in that moment, it didn't matter if I ever got a Game Changers Certification, which I did by the way, after completing the program. But for me, CJ, known as the toughest of the toughest when it comes to feedback, said, "I'm just excited for what the future holds for you." I just needed to put the work ethic in to do it. God gave me something like He gave you, but it's up to us to master it. That's why it's important to get around people who are better than you at what you are aspiring to do. The challenge will raise your performance and make you better.

When I arrived at the airport that day I saw two other coaches from the camp, Kendal Ficklin (a master business coach and speaker) and David Shands (a very successful Entrepreneur). They were waiting at the Delta terminal, so I walked up to coach Kendal and I said, "Coach, thank you." He was the one who calmed my nerves the day before my speech. I was not sure what direction I was supposed to go in for my speech or who my audience was. He said, "Just get up there and be you." I walked over to Coach Kendal at the airport to tell him 'thank you' for just telling me that.

I woke up the next day, I was nervous, sweating bullets, but God was like, 'I got you, you've got to start trusting this gift'. I used to write out speeches. I heard a voice inside me saying, "just write down 10 points and trust me".

Coach Kendal responded to me at the airport saying, "I missed your speech but CJ came out to me right after you were done. He told me, it was a great speech." I was like, okay. David Shands was just over there nodding. I hoped that one day, maybe Kendal would play my presentation for him.

I was at peace because I knew that my life was going in the right direction. I was certain that speaking is what God wanted me to be doing. Had I not invested in myself and went all the way to Michigan, I may not have ever received that much needed revelation. He dangled me above this hot water full of the alligators and said "You're either going to stand tall like a tower or you're going to sink to the summit." It was hard for everybody in my family, outside of my wife, to understand the magnitude of the moment because they weren't there. Still hard to explain to this day. Nevertheless, the memory will forever stay in my heart.

I didn't have any control over the right side of my body. I could tell it to move and it wouldn't move. I had no choice but to be dependent, be patient and cry numerous tears. That sense of loneliness had me looking out the window filled with uncertainty. I saw people laughing and walking through the neighborhood of my parents' house. Still in the same place where I grew up. My friends got great jobs coming out of college. It was the same *wash and repeat* sense of feeling that I felt in alternative school, that same feeling I felt in Pasadena.

I had forgotten that if He's done it before all those other times in my life, then I shouldn't be worried because He will do it again. The challenge is we always want to know how or when everything is going to happen. Because we don't know these things, we feel defeated. That's what I was feeling, when I first made it home from California. I felt so, so defeated.

But when dad got me to therapy, it made me focus on small victories. Therapy makes you literally focus on the ability to make a fist and treasuring that moment like you just bit into a warm savory apple pie. I know therapy with Michael and Dave Tillman taught me patience on a deeper level. I have heard of it, I lived it a little bit, but that experience was real patience.

I just think that when I went through those things and I made my heart ready, that's when God said, "Okay, let's go. I'm about to take you on a journey. The best part about it is you're not going to be around anybody who can counsel you about this journey. You are going to have to leap".

What people don't know about Earl Campbell is that my father was a communications major at the University of Texas. He gave speeches like clockwork. So even if I didn't inherit the power of football, he had passed down an even greater inheritance. My brother didn't get that. My brother is an introvert, he doesn't talk like I do. It's a gift that was always there, I just had to look at life through a different lens. I was looking for football because for me, I thought that I had to walk in the same footsteps as my parents or the people before them. What I didn't realize was that I didn't have to live in a world that wasn't meant for me. Do you believe in fate or destiny? Even through all the hardships, I realized I could overcome it because of my strong will to live. But there's also something uncanny that nobody knows. That fate can play tricks on us. No matter how hard we try to climb, we are destined to fall somewhere, not to continue lying there, but to start climbing again with more strength. If you can just run to the end of the rope without any obstacles, can it be called life? But there is no real ending to the rope that we climb. That is a rope that goes on even after our death, until everyone forgets us.

Everyone told me that in my family, I was the first to be a speaker. I said, "no". But how could they know about the past of my ancestors that even our own family had forgotten. Still, their rope is growing because I remember them. Will the rope ever end? Will there be one day when everyone forgets who we truly were? Wouldn't there be at least one person who will be interested in their ancestors?

CHAPTER 10 "TOUCH-DOWN"

Real Lyfe, Reel Talk.

The slogan, *Real Lyfe, Reel Talk* is what I learned from a man by the name Rodney Page.

Mary B produced an event called Flavors of the Gaslamp in San Diego. The event featured tasting stations donated by the best restaurants in the city. NFL Legends, Eric Allen and Lorenzo Neal were original hosts and we jumped on board to become actively involved. I reached out to my San Diego State teammates and my Father flew in to support and host the event. Due to our NFL connections, we were able to secure noteworthy memorabilia. From there, we get everyone in attendance to bid so we could raise money for Multiple Sclerosis.

I knew that I wanted to do more for scholarships and to do more for research in the MS Community. This was an opportunity, a no brainier to strengthen the cause that I already have a passion for and keep pouring into it. Pro Player Foundation welcomed our family in and we have duplicated a similar event in Austin called "Flavors of Austin".

In our first year, we started out small and it keeps getting better and better. To date, we have hosted 9 Flavors of Austin events and each year thanks to vision and perseverance, we are able to help more people. Collectively, through the help of our supporters, we have put so many kids on scholarships and provided money through the foundation for expanded research. So, I've kept doing the same thing that I was doing in college. Now it serves as our family's way to give back to the MS Community.

I remember when I was in alternative school where people wouldn't necessarily reach us because they would speak over us. They weren't necessarily there for our hearts. As I remember that feeling, I found the nearest alternative school to me, which is in Round Rock, Texas called Success High School. Speaking with the principal, I introduced myself, "My name is Tyler Campbell. I am looking to try to get involved, to try to speak some form of hope and direction into the men who are here." She was happy and replied, "Let me take you to this office of a man by the name of Dr. Rodney Page." I had no idea who Rodney Page was. He looked at me sternly, because they always had people walk in and you never know if somebody's coming into the school that is really there for the kid or their own doing. So he put me through a lot of questions, but he also knew and could see my heart. Mr. Page knew that I was genuine and he knew the product of what I came from. That last name means something, that last name always meant something. When you speak that last name, you can't say anything bad about it because of the pedigree of men and women that it comes from long before, preceding my father, is a good record. So he knew who I was. Not just Earl Campbell's son, I was Ann Campbell's grandson. He said, "I'll be in touch with you."

I got home and hit the Google button to search more about this man, Dr. Rodney Page. I learned he's the first ever women's basketball coach at the University of Texas. He was also the first ever black head coach at the University of Texas (UT). That never gets mentioned in the history books. I had never heard of him; I know UT like the back of my hand. UT had a black women's basketball coach. The more I got to be around him and be in the circle that he called, 'Real Life Real Talk', it was truly something special to witness. It was a safety circle that he engaged with young men in. It was a circle where you can get everything off of your chest in a nonjudgmental environment.

The problems you may have had with the police, your parents not understanding who you are, battles with drug addiction, getting fired, or you try to do the right thing but trouble keeps pulling on you, that was the type of circle that I was able to step in.

Some time had passed and I told Mr. Page I wasn't going to be able to do work with him because I was getting called to do more public speaking. He kindly smiled saying, "You don't have to say that because I always knew that your tenure would not be here for a long time. I knew that you were just supposed to be here so you could get clarity and direction." My dad remembered him from his time at the university. He was amazed and shocked at the same time. He had seen Mr. Page hold Bible studies for athletes on campus when he was in college.

'Real Lyfe Reel Talk' meant something powerful, it hit me differently, so I changed a few things with Mr. Page's blessing. 'Real' stands for transparent and authentic which is everything I strive for as a man. 'LYFE' because there was a song that I used to play like clockwork when I was in college at PCC, by a man named of Lyfe Jennings and it was called 'Must Be Nice'. So I said when I have life I'm going to spell it L-Y-F-E, it was my way of adding my own personal swag to the title while paying homage to Dr. Page as he was a catalyst to my metamorphosis. 'Reel'- everyone's life is a best written novel, a best written movie or a best written story yet to be discovered. 'Talk' because talk is talk and I was blessed with a gift to speak. That's why my radio show is titled "Real Lyfe, Reel Talk."

Even though I use these words to this day, I honor Rodney Page because he gave me the opportunity to utilize his phrase and his slogan. With Mr. Page's blessing the slogan became my mantra.

In my role as a Multiple Sclerosis Ambassador I discovered my newfound purpose which is raising greater awareness for underserved and minority communities that need to know more about MS. My goal is to help break barriers and get black people to see the good in MS clinical trials. A trust that was historically broken in our people largely due to the Tuskegee Experiment of 1932. MS will always be in my heart and for that I must continue to make myself more visible for my community to see.

I was a part of a clinical trial. If we are not a part of clinical research, how do we know if the medications are going to work for people of color? You don't know if you don't have any sample size of research. So that's why I'm always open and letting people know I was a part of a clinical trial, I donated my blood to research.

I must do my part because God told me that as long as I make sure other people are okay with this disease, He's going to make sure that I'm okay. People think I'm crazy when I say that. All I mean by that is He just said from a heart and a mind standpoint, "you'll be okay". To God Be The Glory, I haven't had a relapse with MS since 2011, prior to getting married. I feel that came on me because of so much stress that I had in my life when I hadn't yet learned how to take care of myself. I'm not supposed to be this energetic y'all.

I tell people with pride, MS may take my body but it won't take the words out of my mouth. That is why I'm a speaker, because at the end of the day, this is all I have. Tomorrow all my physical parts can crumble. I know that and I've been through that. Hence, I don't waste any time. I work hard. I don't even let my wife fix my own plate because I know what it's like to not be able to fix a plate. I know what it's like to have everything stripped from me. I know erectile dysfunction, I battle it still to this day and it's been 13 years. I rarely let my wife drive because I know what it's like not to be able to. I give strong hugs to our 3 children Messiah, Cheyenne and Saige because I know what it's like not to hug someone with all of your might. When I say I take the whole 24 hours of a day and soak it up, I take the whole 24. I take it all.

I operate out of a level of fear because I don't want to go back. I just know what it's like to not have. And when you know what it's like not to be able to walk, talk, write, skip or jump, it changes your perspective and outlook on life. Some may think I am koo koo for Cocoa Puffs, but all I am saying is that MS may up and consume my body one day. There may be painful moments when this may even take my eyesight. But as long as I live to serve His children, our Heavenly Father will take care of me.

So speaking for me is not a job, it is fun, it is an honor, and it is a privilege. I give everything that I have, and I don't forget the people who helped me. Rodney Page helped me. He exposed something to me. I used to think that as I grew up in Westlake, nobody would ever hear what I had to say because of the way that I grew up. Mr. Page was the one who told me, "You have a testimony. You have a story. So you tell that doggone story. You tell that story till it makes you blue in the face, because the story is real. People don't want what they can get. Your five steps to do this or eight steps for that. People want to know what have you been through. How did you get through it? That'll speak to black, brown, green, yellow, purple. You let that speak."

I put myself in uncomfortable situations. I've done that for years. I didn't want to speak in churches. I didn't want to speak in the alternative system. That was the first thing I got rushed into. I was so nervous and scared of going to Game Changers in Grand Ledge, MI. Still I faced it.

I'm in the constant motion of just being uncomfortable as a speaker all the time. I don't really fully know the impact, and it's probably my biggest Achilles Heel. I don't necessarily know the impact because I'm so driven to focus on the next thing. I have to work on getting better at that one, because I don't take enough time to rest.

All of you are equipped with everything that you already need, despite your race, your gender, your background, your color, whether you come from money, or not. It's all embedded and it's still in you, but you have to tap into your gift and you have to tap into your purpose in life. When you recognize those things, my brothers, my sisters, not a thing in the world can stop you. Nothing will derail you when you understand who you are, your self-worth, your gift and your purpose; you tapped into what the Divine Man up above gave you.

Uniqueness is actually that 'thing' you feel; it's a plaque over your soul. It's not your worst enemy. You don't have to cry out to change that 'thing' because that's within you. You feel styles so different, that it makes you so much of an outcast, that it marks you so much of a person that does not fit, it is actually that 'thing' that is going to grant you a platform. It's going to give you the stage to tap into the hearts and minds of people across the world.

Hands down, as I look back over my life and think things over, I can truly say that I have had the opportunity to' touch down' without having a football in my hands. Through grace I've had the privilege to reach back and help people who were and are struggling with the same disease I wrestled with. Talk about the power of a touch. When someone else is down, I can stand flat footed, look them dead in the eyes and offer my testimony of hope, no matter what defensive stance they're in. Literally, I know what it is like to not be able to move, yet believe. Now that's putting up true numbers and winning.

CONCLUSION

Life is a huge playbook that is full of audibles but I'm so glad God's been my greatest coach. Even in the times when I didn't know what plays He was calling in from the sidelines of my life, I've learned to trust Him. God is the greatest coach and has a well methodical and strategic plan for my life.

My friend, I realized something valuable that's worth more than its weight in gold. See, I thought as an athlete that if I crossed the end zone line and scored a touchdown for my team, I achieved ultimate success. My belief was rooted in getting my body in the best physical condition so that I could go the distance with the definitive goal of putting six points on the scoreboard.

Little did I know that The Man Up Stairs had a bigger plan than I could have ever conjured up. Although I was fast, God didn't put His gift in my legs because the Lord knew one day, I wouldn't be able to stand on my own. While I was strong and used my hands, biceps and triceps to shed tackles on the field, He didn't place His genius in my arms because the Creator saw that the day would come that I wouldn't be able to move them on my own. The Great Physician didn't place His gift inside my mouth, although I was very fortunate to speak and demand the attention of the masses. My Heavenly Father recognized from eternity that one day my mouth wouldn't be able to move and my tongue would feel like it was glued or tied to the roof of my mouth. Therefore, God placed His endowment inside of the frequency of my voice.

I'm beyond grateful that the pain and body blows of my bouts with MS couldn't stop the pulsating hope and optimism deep down in my heart. My heart is still intact. I truly have victory from the battle despite the scars that are left as roadmaps for others that find themselves in need of finding their way back home to their true selves. Never forget the fact that you can still win even when you fumble the ball. I am living proof. Friends, in times of turmoil, tragedy, and temptations, just retrace the lines of my story.

I just had an epiphany while listening to Jay Z and Mary J Blige 'Can't Knock The Hustle'. I told myself when I first started this book writing process that I'm writing this book for that teenage black boy who I can't stop seeing in my dreams. He's struggling and trying to figure out life but I can never see his face, I can only feel his spirit. Truly, I think that's because the boy that I'm writing the book for is that teenage boy whose heart is still inside of me. I didn't know that when I started this process. I guess if this book wasn't for anyone else, it's for me and served as a form of therapy. My friend, I found myself on every page, each line and between each period of every sentence.

"A Sinner's Prayer"

If you are brave enough to challenge the opposition you face,

Do not be surprised by the fatigue you experience when running your race.

You will become weary, but know simultaneously healing for your soul is taking place.

A blessing will be bestowed upon you, if you are willing to keep the faith.

Life is a test of endurance so it is imperative that you set the right pace.

Therefore, my brothers and my sisters, do not move with such great haste.

Arm yourself with mace.

Trust me, demon repellant will be necessary to check haters and keep them in their place.

So emphatically throw down your ACE.

Shout to the top of your lungs with me, LORD, I AM READY TO CHALLENGE ANY OPPOSITION THAT I AM DESTINED TO FACE.

ABOUT THE AUTHOR

Born October 26, 1986, in Houston, Texas, to Earl and Reuna Campbell. Tyler recalls life-changing words learned from his father at an early age, "A Campbell Never Quits." When confronted with life's obstacles, these words provided strength and encouragement. Tyler received a football scholarship to San Diego State University in 2005. While attending SDSU, he was a consistent scholar athlete and contributed mightily on the gridiron for the Aztecs. The tides of life came rolling in during his junior year when he was diagnosed with Multiple Sclerosis. Tyler became the first individual to play division one college football with the disease. After graduating from SDSU in 2009, Tyler moved back to Austin. He was awarded the honor of becoming a Multiple Sclerosis Ambassador in 2011. An entrepreneur in his own right, Tyler travels the country delivering empowering, inspiring and motivating messages of resiliency and self-worth. Coining the phrase "TC Speaks", Tyler hosts his own on air radio show every Saturday from 12pm-1pm CST on 104.9 The Horn FM in Austin. Tyler, his wife Shana and their 3 children reside in Texas.

For More Information or To Book Tyler:

Web: www.iamtylercampbell.com

YouTubeChannel: youtube.com/c/TCSpeaks

https://soundcloud.app.goo.gl/VnJ47Fh5Cm83V6yRA

TESTIMONIALS

I've known Tyler Campbell since his playing days at San Diego State and one thing that always stood out to me was his passion. He was always more than his family football legacy. At such a young age he's been able to take his life experiences and turn them into teachable and relatable moments that help to inspire those around them to be there best. Tyler is a man of faith and isn't afraid to share his belief.

Akbar Gbajabiamila
American Ninja Warrior Host

Tyler, it's difficult to move mountains if you've never encountered one. The obstacles you have overcome at such a young age have aided in the construction of the man you have become. Your life experience serves as a beacon of inspiration for anyone who has faced adversity in their journey. Sharing your message of triumph with others is obviously your calling and it continues to provide a blueprint to fulfillment for people of all ages.

Ced Golden
Austin American-Statesman Sports Columnist

Tyler Campbell is one of the humblest and salt of the earth people I have ever met. He is a highly principled and selfless man. Being in his presence increases your zest for life. Tyler's authentic thirst for lifting others is unparalleled. Clearly, the world needs more human beings like Tyler Campbell ~ he is truly the gold standard!

Dr. Michael McClellan
Chaffey College, Senior Administrator

I have known Tyler since he was a running back at San Diego State. When practice had concluded and all of his teammates were headed to the showers, Tyler would be running wind sprints with a tire in tow. His positive attitude, work ethic and his faith in God is alive today! Thanks, Tyler! This is a must read for all!

Coach Del Miller (Retired)
Former San Diego State Offensive Coordinator

"I think Tyler has a super powerful story and message, not just for the community at large, but for the MS Community. He injects humor into his speech and that's amazing. Tyler broke his message down for non-football people in a really funny way. That's the highest form of compliment I can give. I just enjoyed it, bro. I didn't even have feedback. It was great."

CJ Quinney
Eric Thomas & Associates "Game Changers Speaker Program"

He really caught my attention. Tyler, I feel like you're a natural on stage, it just fits with you. When engaging in conversation with Tyler or to hear him speak to the audience, I forgot he and I had a conversation earlier about MS. But when he set up his speech the way that he set it up, I was like, 'Oh, boom'. All right! Tyler had us when he created that tension for a while, so we were paying attention. Then when you hit home with that issue, 'It was like oh, okay, cool', then Tyler let it ride out. He gave the points to his keynote and his delivery was powerful. Tyler is my favorite type of speaker because I don't even watch with a critical eye. Not even two seconds in, I stopped watching it and was like, "How can I give him feedback? Tyler, it's just like you have something that you can't really teach."

Kantis Simmons
Eric Thomas & Associates "Game Changers Speaker Program"